First World War
and Army of Occupation
War Diary
France, Belgium and Germany

GUARDS DIVISION
1 Guards Brigade
Headquarters
1 December 1916 - 31 December 1916

WO95/1213/3

The Naval & Military Press Ltd
www.nmarchive.com
Published in association with The National Archives

Published by

The Naval & Military Press Ltd

Unit 10 Ridgewood Industrial Park,

Uckfield, East Sussex,

TN22 5QE England

Tel: +44 (0) 1825 749494

www.naval-military-press.com

www.nmarchive.com

This diary has been reprinted in facsimile from the original. Any imperfections are inevitably reproduced and the quality may fall short of modern type and cartographic standards.

© **Crown Copyright**
Images reproduced by permission of The National Archives, London, England, 2015.

Contents

Document type	Place/Title	Date From	Date To
Heading	WO95/1213 Dec 1916.		
War Diary	Sandpits Camp E.24.d	01/12/1916	08/12/1916
War Diary	Sandpits Camp	09/12/1916	15/12/1916
War Diary	Sandpits To Combles Catacombs	16/12/1916	17/12/1916
War Diary	Combles	18/12/1916	31/12/1916
Miscellaneous	G.D. No. 2569/1/G.	19/11/1916	19/11/1916
Miscellaneous	Guards Division Defence Scheme.		
Miscellaneous	Boundaries.		
Miscellaneous	Appendix "A" Gas Attack.		
Miscellaneous	Appendix "B". S.O.S.		
Miscellaneous	Appendix "C". Medical Arrangements In The Event Of Hostile Attack.		
Miscellaneous	Appendix "D". Gas Alert.		
Map	Guards Divn. H.Q.		
Miscellaneous	1st Guards Brigade No 805/1.	16/12/1916	16/12/1916
Miscellaneous	1st G.B. No. 713.	03/12/1916	03/12/1916
Miscellaneous	Defence Scheme For The Divisional Reserve Of Guards Division.	03/12/1916	03/12/1916
Miscellaneous	Battalions In Back Area Forming Divisional Reserve.		
Miscellaneous	1st G.B. No. 713.	03/12/1916	03/12/1916
Miscellaneous	Defence Scheme For The Divisional Reserve Of Guards Division.	03/12/1916	03/12/1916
Operation(al) Order(s)	1st Guards Brigade Order No. 93.	16/12/1916	16/12/1916
Miscellaneous	Daily Intelligence Report 1st Guards Brigade.	17/12/1916	17/12/1916
Operation(al) Order(s)	1st Guards Brigade Order No. 93.	16/12/1916	16/12/1916
Miscellaneous	Trench Roster.		
Miscellaneous	1st G.B. No. 914.	30/12/1916	30/12/1916
Miscellaneous	1st G.B. No. 801/1.	16/12/1916	16/12/1916
Miscellaneous	Instructions No. 1 For Right Group.		
Miscellaneous	Instructions No. 3 For Right Group.	17/12/1916	17/12/1916
Miscellaneous	Instructions No. 4 For Right Group.	19/12/1916	19/12/1916
Miscellaneous	Daily Intelligence Report-1st Guards Brigade. 8 A.M. Decr. 17th To 8 A.M. Decr. 18th.	17/12/1916	17/12/1916
Miscellaneous	Daily Intelligence Report-1st Guards Brigade. 8 A.M. Decr. 18th To 8 A.M. Decr. 19th.	18/12/1916	18/12/1916
Miscellaneous	Daily Intelligence Report. 1st Guards Bde. 8 a.m. Decr. 19th 1916 To 8 a.m. Decr. 20th 1916.	19/12/1916	19/12/1916
Miscellaneous	Instructions No.6 For Right Group.	20/12/1916	20/12/1916
Miscellaneous	Daily Intelligence Report, 1st Guards Brigade. 8 a.m. Decr. 20th 1916-8 a.m. Decr. 21st 1916.	20/12/1916	20/12/1916
Operation(al) Order(s)	1st Guards Brigade Order No. 94.	21/12/1916	21/12/1916
Miscellaneous	Daily Intelligence Report, 1st Guards Brigade. 8 a.m. Decr. 21st 1916 To 8 a.m. Decr. 22nd 1916.	21/12/1916	21/12/1916
Miscellaneous	Daily Intelligence Report, 1st Guards Brigade. 8 a.m. Decr. 22nd 1916 To 8 a.m. Decr. 23rd 1916.	22/12/1916	22/12/1916
Miscellaneous	Defence Scheme Right Guards Brigade Group.		
Map	Guards Div. H.Q. 20.12.16.		
Miscellaneous		23/12/1916	23/12/1916
Miscellaneous	Appendix "A". Principles Of Defence.		
Miscellaneous	Appendix "B". Gas Alert.		

Miscellaneous	1st G.B. No. 922.	23/12/1916	23/12/1916
Miscellaneous	Defence Scheme Right Guards Brigade Group.	23/12/1916	23/12/1916
Miscellaneous	Appendix "A". Principles Of Defence.		
Miscellaneous	Appendix "B". Gas Alert.		
Miscellaneous	Daily Intelligence Report 1st Guards Brigade. 8 A.M. Decr. 23rd To 8 A.M. Decr. 24th.	23/12/1916	23/12/1916
Miscellaneous	Daily Intelligence Report, 1st Guards Brigade. 8 a.m. Decr. 24th 1916 To 8 a.m. Decr. 25th 1916.	24/12/1916	24/12/1916
Miscellaneous	Daily Intelligence Report-1st Guards Bde., 8 A.M. Decr. 25th To 8 A.M. Decr. 26th.	25/12/1916	25/12/1916
Miscellaneous	Daily Intelligence Report. 1st Guards Bde. 8 A.M. Decr. 26th To 8 A.M. Decr. 27th.	26/12/1916	26/12/1916
Operation(al) Order(s)	Warning Order. Guards Division Order No. 101.	26/12/1916	26/12/1916
Miscellaneous	Daily Intelligence Report-1st Guards Brigade. 8 A.M. Decr. 27th To 8 A.M. Decr. 28th.	27/12/1916	27/12/1916
Miscellaneous	Daily Intelligence Report-1st Guards Bde. 8 A.M. Dec: 29th To 8 A.M. Dec: 30th.	29/12/1916	29/12/1916
Operation(al) Order(s)	Guards Division Order No. 102.	26/12/1916	26/12/1916
Miscellaneous	Appendix "A". Movements Of Battalions Of Guards Division During Relief.		
Miscellaneous	Distribution Of Guards Brigades On Completion Of Relief. Appendix "B".		
Miscellaneous	G.D. No. 2674/G.	28/12/1916	28/12/1916
Miscellaneous	Appendix "C"		
Miscellaneous	Daily Intelligence Report-1st Guards Bde., 8 A.M. Decr. 28th To 8 A.M. Decr. 29th.	28/12/1916	28/12/1916
Operation(al) Order(s)	1st Guards Brigade Order No. 95.	29/12/1916	29/12/1916
Miscellaneous			
Operation(al) Order(s)	Guards Division Order No. 103.	31/12/1916	31/12/1916
Miscellaneous	Movements Of Battalions Of Guards Division During Relief. Appendix "A".		
Miscellaneous	Distribution Of Guards Brigades On Completion Of Relief. Appendix "B".		
Miscellaneous	Appendix "C"		
Miscellaneous	G.D. No. 2679/G.	30/12/1916	30/12/1916
Miscellaneous	1st Guards Brigade.	29/12/1916	29/12/1916
Miscellaneous	1st G.B. No. 996.	27/12/1916	27/12/1916
Miscellaneous	Movements Of Battalions Of Guards Division During Relief.		
Miscellaneous	1st Guards Brigade Intelligence Report. 8 a.m. 30th Decr. To 8 a.m. 31st Decr.	30/12/1916	30/12/1916
Miscellaneous	Amendment to 1st Guards Brigade Order No. 95.	01/01/1917	01/01/1917
Miscellaneous	Intelligence Report, 1st Guards Brigade. 8 a.m. 31st Decr. 1916 To 1st January 1917.	31/12/1916	31/12/1916
Miscellaneous	1st G.B. No. 996.	27/12/1916	27/12/1916
Miscellaneous	Movements Of Battalions Of Guards Division During Relief.		
Miscellaneous	Handing Over Notes.	31/12/1916	31/12/1916
Miscellaneous	Please Destroy Instructions No 5 For Right Group At Present In Your Possession.		
Miscellaneous	Amendment Instructions No. 5 For Right Group.	23/12/1916	23/12/1916
Miscellaneous	Instructions No. 6 for Right Group.	20/12/1916	20/12/1916
Miscellaneous	Instructions No. 7 for Right Group.	23/12/1916	23/12/1916
Miscellaneous	Right Group. Instructions For Sapping Platoons.	20/12/1916	20/12/1916

WO95
1213
Dec 1916

WAR DIARY or INTELLIGENCE SUMMARY

Army Form C. 2118.

(Erase heading not required.)

December 1916 1st Guards Bde.

Place	Date	Hour	Summary of Events and Information	Remarks and references to Appendices
SANDPITS cont. E.24.d	Dec 1st	11.30 a.m.	Conference at Bde H.Q. by C.O.O. Hand grenades.	
	Dec 2nd		3rd Cold. Gds moved from FORKED TREE camp to MALTZHORN FARM. A.2.a. 2nd Gren Gds moved from MEAULTE to Camp 108, BRONFAY. Bde. Div. Defence Scheme received.	AH 265
	Dec 3rd	10.30 P.M.	3rd Cold. Gds moved from MALTZHORN FARM into the line taking over from the 152nd French Division. 1st Irish Gds moved from FORKED TREE to MALTZHORN 2nd Cold. Gds moved from MEAULTE to COMBLES M.G. Coy & T.M. Battery moved from SANDPITS to MANSEL CAMP. These moves were made in accordance with orders issued by G.O.C. 2nd Gds Bde. the Right group commander, the Right group consisting of the 2nd Gds Bde. & 1st Batn Cold Gds & 2nd Irish Gds of the 2nd Gds Bde. G.O.C. 1st Gds Bde took over command of Divisional Reserve, consisting of two batts of each group in the back area, & recvd M.G. Coy & T.M. Battery.	
		8 P.M.	1st Gds Bde Defence Scheme issued to all Batts concerned.	

266

WAR DIARY
or
INTELLIGENCE SUMMARY

Army Form C. 2118.

Place	Date	Hour	Summary of Events and Information	Remarks and references to Appendices
Sandpits camp E.24.d.	Dec 4th		2nd Gren Gds moved into our gds to our this camp at BRONFAY FM.	
	5th		3rd Coldstream Gds relieved in line by a Bn. of 3rd Gds Bde - & withdrawn to MALTZ HORN Camp.	
	6th		3rd Coldstream Gds moved to BRONFAY Farm 2nd Gren Gds " " MALTZ HORN " 2nd Colds Gds " " " 1st Scots Gds " " Rgt Left Subsector Right " " " SAILLY SAILLISEL	
	7th		Bde Bombing Officer started a bombing school for Reserve Bns at BRONFAY FARM.	
	8th	12 noon	Casualties 2nd Colds Gds O.R. wounded 1. 1st Scots Gds O.R. " 2. 1st Coldstream relieved 2nd Coldstream in left Sub Sector - 2nd Coldstream moving to MALTZHORN Camp. 2nd Gren Gds moved from MALTZ HORN to COMBLES area. The weather again became wet & the going began to become bad -	

Army Form C. 2118.

WAR DIARY
or
INTELLIGENCE SUMMARY
(Erase heading not required.)

Instructions regarding War Diaries and Intelligence Summaries are contained in F. S. Regs., Part II. and the Staff Manual respectively. Title Pages will be prepared in manuscript.

Place	Date	Hour	Summary of Events and Information	Remarks and references to Appendices
SAND PITS Camp	Dec 9th		2nd Gren Gds relieved 1st Irish Gds in rt subsector.	
			1st Gldy Gds moved into BRONFAY Camp	
			3rd Cold Gds " " COMBLES area	
		12 noon	Casualties: 2nd Gren Gds. O.R. W. 1	
			1st Irish Gds " 5	
	Dec 10th		3rd Cold Gds relieved 1st Cold Gds	
			2nd Irish Gds moved into COMBLES	
			1st Irish Gds moved into Camp H.	
			1st C.G. moved to MALTZHORN Fm.	
		12 noon	Casualties: 1st Irish Gds - O.R. K. 2. wounded 2	
	Dec 11th		2nd Irish Gds relieved 2nd Gren Gds	
			1st Gren Gds to MALTZHORN Camp	
			2nd Cold Gds to COMBLES area	
			1st Cold Gds to BRONFAY Fm	
		12 noon	Casualties: 2nd Cold Gds O.R. wounded killed 2	
			3rd Cold Gds " wounded 2	
	Dec 12th		2nd Cold Gds relieved	
			1st Irish Gds to COMBLES area	
			2nd Gds Bde to MALTZHORN Camp	
			Casualties 2nd Gren Gds. O.R. K. 1. W. 3. M. 2	
			2nd Cold Gds. 2.O. K. 7. W. 7 (one killed)	
			Capt S.E. Rose. R.A.M.C. wounded at duty	

WAR DIARY
or
INTELLIGENCE SUMMARY

(Erase heading not required.)

Army Form C. 2118.

Place	Date	Hour	Summary of Events and Information	Remarks and references to Appendices
SANDPITS Camp	Dec 13	12 m.n.	Casualties 2nd Coldstream Gds. Officers wounded – Lt. C. BERKELEY. 2/Lt T.H. PORRITT. O.R. K. 1. wounded 3. Missing 1. 3rd Coldstream Gds. O.R. wounded 1. 1st Scots Gds. 2. Coy. O.R. Killed 2. wounded 1. 1st Irish Gds. do. moved to MAITZHORN camp – 3rd Colds Gds. moved to BRENTAY camp – N – 1 Coldstream Gds. moved to COMBLES area –	
	Dec.14.		1. C.G relieved 2 C.G who moved to MAITZHORN camp. 2 S.G moved to BRENTAY camp 10.5. – 2 I.G moved from w. corner to camp to COMBLES area – H Camp carried to be H. Camp of S.G. Gds Div. 2nd Colds. Gds. Casualties O.R. wounded 6 (2 at duty) 1st Irish Gds O.R. wounded 4 at duty	
	Dec.15.		Weather still wet + overcast – Casualties 2nd Grenr. Gds O.R. wounded 1. M.I. believed killed 2nd Colds. Gds O.R. killed 1. wounded 2. 1st Irish Gds O.R. wounded 5.	

Army Form C. 2118.

WAR DIARY
or
INTELLIGENCE SUMMARY
(*Erase heading not required.*)

Instructions regarding War Diaries and Intelligence Summaries are contained in F. S. Regs., Part II. and the Staff Manual respectively. Title Pages will be prepared in manuscript.

Place	Date	Hour	Summary of Events and Information	Remarks and references to Appendices
SANDPITS to COMBLES Catacombs	Dec 16th	10.45am	Conference of Brigadiers at 3rd Infl. Bde H.Q. 9 questions discussed	
		12 noon	Bde H.Q. took over from 2nd Inf. Bde H.Q.	267
			3rd Coldstream Gds relieved 1st Essex Regt. in left sub-sector - 1st C.G. moved to MAURIZ HORN camp	269
			2nd Grenadier Gds moved up to COMBLES area	270
			1st Grenadier Gds moved from MAURIZ HORN camp to BRITTANY camp	268
		12 noon	Casualties: 2nd Grenadier Gds 2 O.R. wounded. 1st Brick Gds 2 killed. 1 wounded.	
		8pm	1st Pdl. Bde Order No 93 issued	
			Instructions No 1 issued to Units	
	Dec 17th	4 am	Situation normal -	
		8 am	Instructions No 2 issued.	
		12 noon	Casualties NIL.	
			Intelligence	269
				see APP 269
		2pm	For relief see up to Instructions No 3 issued	271

WAR DIARY or INTELLIGENCE SUMMARY

Army Form C. 2118.

Place	Date	Hour	Summary of Events and Information	Remarks and references to Appendices
COMBLES	Dec 18th		A very quiet day - nothing to report - Intelligence see 400	272
		12 noon	Casualties 2nd Grenadier Gds O.R. killed 1. 3rd Coldstream Gds O.R. wounded 3.	
"	19th		During the night there was a frost which improved the going & added materially to the comfort of the troops -	
		12 noon	Casualties 2nd Coldstream Gds O.R. wounded 1. 3rd " Gds " " 1. 2nd Irish Gds " " 1.	
		"	Instructions No 4 issued	Intelligence 273, 274
		6 pm	Instructions No 5 issued	275
"	20th	12 noon	Casualties 2nd Coldstream Gds O.R. wounded 1. 1st Irish Gds O.R. " 2 (1 self inflicted)	
			The day was the first clear one for some time with the result that there was much aeroplane activity but hostile shelling was not increased. Instructions No 6 issued. Intelligence	276, 277

Army Form C. 2118.

WAR DIARY
or
INTELLIGENCE SUMMARY

(Erase heading not required.)

Instructions regarding War Diaries and Intelligence Summaries are contained in F.S. Regs., Part II. and the Staff Manual respectively. Title Pages will be prepared in manuscript.

Place	Date	Hour	Summary of Events and Information	Remarks and references to Appendices
COMBLES	Dec 21st	12 noon	Casualties. 2nd Bn Pbs. O.R. Killed. (Previously reported missing on 11.12.15) 1.O.R. 1st Coldm. Gds killed. Capt. R.L.C. BEWICKE - COPLEY.	
		2pm	Enemy artillery & aeroplanes more active again. 1st Bn Bde Order No 94 issued.	278 Intelligence 279
	Dec 22nd	12 noon	Casualties Nil. Very quiet day – a bombardment which was to have been carried out in the morning was postponed on account of the bad weather.	280 Intelligence
	Dec 23rd		Casualties. 2nd Coldm Bn. O.R. died. 3rd Coldm Bn. 1 Killed. A Coy which attempted to work on the intermediate line was interfered with by hostile shelling. Defence Scheme issued.	281 Intelligence 281/A
	Dec 24th	12 noon	Casualties – 2nd Scots Gds killed. 1 wounded. 3rd Coldm Gds - 1 - 1 2nd Grenr Gds - 1 - 2	
		9pm	A clear day. Our aeroplanes somewhat active – enemy's left which carried an artillery group of 4 pieces a few rounds on the enemy to retaliate on smeary countries.	282 Intelligence

2449 S.B. ᴗ/ᴗ J.B.C. & A./Forms/C.2118/12.

WAR DIARY
or
INTELLIGENCE SUMMARY

Army Form C. 2118.

Place	Date	Hour	Summary of Events and Information	Remarks and references to Appendices
COMBLES	Dec 25th	8.30am to 8.45am	Artillery carried out a short sharp bombardment. Enemy retaliated	
		11.30am to 11.45am	by shelling SAILLY-SAILLISEL mostly along the main RAPHENZ road.	
		12 noon	so that little damage was done -	223 Intelligence
			Casualties. 2nd Colds Gds. O.R. wounded - 3. (1 at duty)	
			3rd Colds Gds O.R " 1	
			2nd Irish Gds O.R Killed 1. wounded 2.	
	Dec 26th		A very large amount of aerial activity - several enemy planes	
			of both sides brought down.	284 Intelligence
		12 noon	Casualties. 2nd Colds Gds O.R. wounded. 1.	
			1st Irish Gds O.R " 1	
			2nd Irish Gds O.R " 2 (1 at duty)	
		1pm to 4pm	Bombardment by enemy TMs carried on from our artillery with apparently good results - little retaliation -	
			Brig General C.E. PEREIRA left the Bde to take over command of the 2nd Division -	
			Lt Col. R.M. M.C. CALMONT 1st Bn Irish Gds assumed temporary command of the Bde.	
	Dec 27th	12 noon	Casualties 2nd Coldstream Gds. O.R. Killed 1.	
			1st Irish Gds O.R wounded 4 (2 at duty)	
			1st Bn Bde L.T.Coy. O.R. wounded 1.	

WAR DIARY
or
INTELLIGENCE SUMMARY
(Erase heading not required.)

Army Form C. 2118.

Place	Date	Hour	Summary of Events and Information	Remarks and references to Appendices
COMBLES	Dec 27th		The day was a very fine one & there was a certain amount of artillery activity on both sides. Casualties.	286. 285/a
		12 noon		Intelligence 8th Division Order No. 161 received
	Dec 28th		A quiet day. There were several degrees of frost during the night of 27/28th but a thaw & rain set in during this afternoon rendering the conditions almost as bad again as they had been three weeks before.	286 286/a Intelligence 8th Division Order No. 102 & attendix received
			Casualties. 1st Cold. Gds. O.R. killed 1. Signallers 2. 2nd Irish Gds. O.R. wounded 1.	
		12 noon	Casualties. 3rd Cold. Rgt. O.R. wounded 1. 3rd Gds. Rgt. " " 1. 1st Irish Rgt. " " 4.	
	Dec 29th	12 noon		287
		2.45 p.m	The heavy artillery & field artillery carried out a bombardment of the German trenches M.11.14.6.	Intelligence

Army Form C. 2118.

WAR DIARY
or
INTELLIGENCE SUMMARY
(Erase heading not required.)

Instructions regarding War Diaries and Intelligence Summaries are contained in F.S. Regs., Part II. and the Staff Manual respectively. Title Pages will be prepared in manuscript.

Place	Date	Hour	Summary of Events and Information	Remarks and references to Appendices
COMBLES	Dec 29th	6.35pm	2nd Gds Bde Order No. 95 issued.	Appx. 288.
	Dec 30th	12 n'n	~~Operations~~ The enemy artillery were very active throughout the morning — especially in the neighbourhood of SAILLY SAILLISEL & church of GUEUDECOURT. The Reserve line of Left Bn in N.7.d. was heavily shelled from 10 a.m. to 12.30 p.m., a certain amount of damage being done to the trench. Our trenches had again become very wet & little headway could be made. Intelligence	289
			1st Cold. Gds. Lt. J.N.C. WHITAKER ~~was~~ wounded, attacked Bde W.D.	
			3rd Cold. Gds. O.R. killed 2.	
			2nd Irish Gds. O.R. wounded 1. Lt. R.G. JENSON wounded.	
			2nd Gds Bde In'd Coy O.R. killed 1.	

Army Form C. 2118.

WAR DIARY
or
INTELLIGENCE SUMMARY
(Erase heading not required.)

Place	Date	Hour	Summary of Events and Information	Remarks and references to Appendices
COMBLES	Dec 31	12 noon	Casualties. 2nd Coldstream Gds — O.R. wounded 1. 2nd Irish Gds — O.R. wounded 2. Brig General G.D. JEFFREYS. C.M.G. assumed command of the Brigade. A quiet day. 1/1/17	App. 290. Intelligence.

Jas. Ester Bar
Brig General
Commg 1st Guards Bde.

SECRET

Copy No. 5

G.D. No. 2569/1/G.

1st Guards Brigade

Herewith Guards Division Defence Scheme.

Provisional Defence Scheme, G.D. No.2569/G, is cancelled.

Paragraphs in which attached Defence Scheme differs from the Provisional Scheme are marked in Red.

A C K N O W L E D G E.

C P Heywood
Lieut-Colonel,
General Staff. Guards Divn.

19th December 1916.

Copy No. 1   General Staff.
    2   "Q".
    3   G.D.A.
    4   C.R.E.
    5   1st Guards Brigade.
    6   2nd Guards Brigade.
    7   3rd Guards Brigade.
    8   Pioneer Battalion.
    9   A.D.M.S.
   10   XIV Corps.
   11   20th Division.
   12   4th Division.
   13   War Diary.

****

SECRET

G.D. No.2569/1/G.

GUARDS DIVISION DEFENCE SCHEME.

1. Boundaries.
2. Organisation of Defence.
3. Distribution of Infantry.
4. Artillery Support.
5. Principles of Defence.
6. Distribution of Machine Guns.
7. Divisional Reserve.

APPENDICES.

A. Gas Attack.
B. S. O. S.
C. Medical Arrangements in case of Attack.

Map shewing Defensive Lines and Boundaries.

2.

1. **BOUNDARIES.**

    The front to be held by the Division extends from U.14.B.9.6 to T.6.B.7.2.

    Boundaries of Divisional Area.

    Divisional Boundaries and inter-sector Boundaries are shewn on attached map.

2. **ORGANISATION OF DEFENCE.**

    The defensive system will be organised as follows:-

    A. Front line system of fire and support trenches.

    B. The Reserve Line as shown on attached map.

    C. A switch line consisting of strong points on the general line SAILLY-SAILLISEL CHURCH - U.13.Central - MOUCHOIR COPSE for the protection of the right flank of the Division.

    D. The Intermediate Line as shewn on map attached.

    E. The 2nd Line as shewn on map attached (not yet constructed).

    F. Defended localities at the N.E. extremity of COMBLES - and at LEUZE WOOD (not yet constructed).

3. **DISTRIBUTION OF INFANTRY.**

    Right Sector.

Right Guards Brigade Group) Headquarters.)		COMBLES CATACOMBS.
2 Battalions	-	(Front system, Reserve Line, and trenches about NORTH COPSE (U.7.c).
1 Battalion	-	In area HAIE WOOD - COMBLES.
1 Battalion	-	In MALTZHORN FARM.
2 Battalions	-	Back area.

    /Left

Left Sector.

Left Guards Brigade Group Headquarters.		T.26.a.10.2.
2 Battalions	-	In front system & Reserve Line.
1 Battalion	-	In area BOULEAUX WOOD and T.26.B.
1 Battalion	-	MALTZHORN FARM.
2 Battalions	-	Back area.

4. ARTILLERY SUPPORT.

(a)   The Divisional front is supported by the Divisional Artillery which is divided into two Groups - one Group supporting each Guards Brigade Sector.

Hd.Qrs. Right Group	COMBLES, T.28.A.7.3.
Hd. Qrs. Left Group	T.26.A.10.2.

(b)   Support of Heavy Artillery will be called for through Divisional Headquarters or Divisional Artillery Headquarters.

5. PRINCIPLES OF DEFENCE.

The following principles will be adopted in holding the line:-

(a)   The front line will be held as thinly as is consistent with security. To permit of thus holding the front line, good wire entanglements are necessary, good arrangements for flank defence, and close and continuous observation on the part of Artillery F.O.Os.

(b)   Troops will NOT fall back from one line to any other line, but all ground will be defended as long as possible whether the flanks are turned or not.

(c)   There are three kinds of attack which may be anticipated:-

((1)

(i) A raid.

(ii) An attack on a minor scale to capture some locality, accompanied by a bombardment.

(iii) A serious attack preceded by a heavy bombardment.

(d) <u>As regards (c) (i)</u> :- Vigilance, active patrolling, combined with a good system of listening posts and wire, make the failure of such attacks certain.

(e) <u>As regards (c) (ii)</u> :- Should the enemy succeed in establishing himself in our trenches, he should be counter attacked immediately from both flanks and from the support trenches where such are in sufficiently close proximity.

The extent and intensity of the enemy's bombardment if closely observed, should give an indication of his objective and enable preparations for counter attack to be made before his attack is delivered. The essential is to deny him time in which to consolidate.

Should the counter attack fail, the captured portion of our trenches must be isolated by blocking, and support trenches firmly held until more deliberate preparations can be made.

Meanwhile, the Artillery will prevent German reinforcements crossing "No Man's Land", and the Infantry must do their utmost to reconnoitre and locate the exact position held by the enemy, so that our Artillery may bombard the captured trenches with precision: thus further counter attack by our reserves will be executed under the most favourable conditions.

Artillery fire will not be opened on the captured trenches without the sanction of the Guards Brigadier concerned.

/(f)

5.

(f) <u>As regards (c) (iii)</u> :- It is unlikely that such an attack will come as a surprise, and Commanders will have time to make suitable dispositions.

In any case, no good will be gained by reinforcing the front line.

Supporting troops must hold their ground, and by means of fire and local attacks keep the enemy in check until sufficient reserves are available to assume the offensive.

(g) All Officers must consider the action to be taken by the troops under their command in the event of attack on any portion of the front for the defence of which they are responsible. Plans must be thought out beforehand, and the action to be taken known to all. Nothing should be left to chance.

Brigades, Battalions and Companies must keep each other informed of their plans to meet various eventualities.

6. <u>DISTRIBUTION OF MACHINE GUNS.</u>

(a) Right and Left Guards Brigade Groups will each maintain 2 machine guns in the Intermediate Line.

Right Guards Brigade Group will maintain 2 machine guns in strong point T.28.B.8.4.

(b) G.Os.C. Guards Brigade Groups will mention in their Defence Schemes the action, in case of attack, of such machine guns of the Machine Gun Company supporting their fronts as are normally in reserve and not included in the defensive organisation of the 2nd Line or more advanced positions.

/7.

7. **DIVISIONAL RESERVE.**

    (a)   The Divisional Reserve will be composed of the following troops under command of   Guards Brigadier in reserve.

        Machine Gun Company in reserve.

        Light Trench Mortar Battery in reserve.

        2 Battalions Right Group in back area.

        2 Battalions Left Group in back area.

    (b)   In case of attack, Divisional Reserve will be prepared to move on receipt of orders to MALTZHORN CAMP, Reserve Brigade Hd.Qrs. will be prepared to move to Divisional Hd.Qrs. at ARROWHEAD COPSE on receipt of orders.

    (c)   O.C. Brigade Machine Gun Company in reserve will reconnoitre the Intermediate and 2nd line, with a view to being able to push forward guns to reinforce these lines of defence if so ordered.

****

APPENDIX "A".

GAS ATTACK.

In case of a "GAS ATTACK", the alarm will be spread by every available means.

Telephone operators will send "GAS" to all concerned.

Infantry, Lewis guns, and machine guns will open a steady regulated fire on the German trenches.

Artillery will open a deliberate fire on the German trenches and get ready for rapid barrage in case of of receipt of "S.O.S." message, or on seeing the "S.O.S." rocket signal.

NOTE. In spreading the alarm for Gas Shell bombardments, Strombus Horns, Gongs, and other signals for a gas attack will not be employed.

****

APPENDIX "B".

S. O. S.

The "S.O.S." telephone message or "S.O.S." rocket signal, means that the Germans are actually leaving their trenches to attack, and that rapid barrage is required from guns and from machine guns that can barrage in front of our front line.

****

APPENDIX "C".

MEDICAL ARRANGEMENTS IN THE EVENT OF HOSTILE ATTACK.

All existing arrangements are made and worked daily in view of the contingency of hostile attack.

POSITIONS OF ADVANCED DRESSING STATIONS AND BEARER POSTS.

(a) A.D.Ss. at (i) COMBLES CATACOMBS.
             (ii) Forward A.D.S. at T.17.d.7.3.
(b) Car loading post at T.23.b.9.7.
(c) Bearer (Relay) Posts:-

Left Sector.

(1) T.12.a.5.9 in conjunction with a Battalion Aid Post.
(2) U.7.c.5.9 in conjunction with a Battalion Aid Post.
(3) T.18.a.5.9.

Right Sector.

U.13.a.3.5 in conjunction with a Battalion Aid Post.

POSITION OF BATTALION AID POSTS.

Left Sector.   T.12.a.5.9.
                   U.7.c.5.9.

Right Sector. U.13.a.3.5.
                   U.14.a.1.7., at Chateau.

POSITION OF RESERVE BEARER DIVISIONS (2) A.6.b.8.4.

FRONT LINE CLEARANCE.

(a) Under normal conditions.

(i) Left Sector. Battalion stretcher bearers clear the front line to Battalion Aid Posts, and also convey casualties to Ambulance Bearer Post at T.18.a.5.9, with assistance of ambulance bearer squads posted at Battalion Aid Posts, if necessary. The Bearer Post at T.18.a.5.9 is cleared by ambulance bearers to forward A.D.S. at T.17.d.7.3. After receiving further surgical attention - hot drinks etc. - here, the cases are carried by stretcher bearers to Loading Post at T.23.b.9.7, and placed in ambulance cars and conveyed to A.D.S. at COMBLES.

(ii) Right Sector. Battalion stretcher bearers clear the front line to Battalion Aid Posts. The stretcher bearers of the Right Battalion of this Sector clear their Aid Post to U.13.a.3.5, where ambulance bearers relieve them and convey casualties to forward A.D.S. at T.17.d.7.3.

(iii) A Tent and Bearer Division are normally employed in daily clearance, with two Bearer Divisions in Reserve. Three ambulance cars are employed between Loading Post and A.D.S. at COMBLES. The A.D.S. at COMBLES is also cleared by these cars to TRONES WOOD A.D.S. (under XIV Corps administration). Additional cars are obtained from O.C. TRONES WOOD A.D.S. when required. The TRONES WOOD A.D.S. is cleared by M.A.C. to C.C.S.

MEDICAL ARRANGEMENTS IN THE EVENT OF HOSTILE ATTACK. (Contd).

(b) **In the event of hostile attack.**

The forward A.D.S. and Bearer Posts will be reinforced to the extent of one Bearer Division. Bearer Squads will be pushed forward to Battalion Aid Posts to assist the Battalion Medical Officers in clearing their Aid Posts. Horsed ambulance wagons, in addition to extra ambulance cars, will be employed from Loading Post to A.D.S. at COMBLES and from there to TRONES WOOD A.D.S. if necessary. A Bearer Division and 6 horsed ambulance wagons will be held in readiness to be employed as the situation dictates.

****

APPENDIX "D".

GAS ALERT.

When the wind is between N.W. and S.E. Guards Brigades in the line will send the message "ALERT" to all units under their command, also to supporting Artillery Group and other attached units.

The extra precautions to be taken on receipt of this message are as follows:-

EXTRA PRECAUTIONS TO BE TAKEN DURING A GAS ALERT.

1. All men in positions where they are liable to be suddenly overwhelmed by gas will wear their helmets rolled up and pinned on front of the coat (as per instructions G.D. 1566/G).

2. A sentry will be posted on every tunnel dugout, or other dugout holding more than 10 men.

3. A sentry will be posted on each group of two or three small dugouts.

4. A sentry will be posted on each Headquarters and Signal Office.

5. Men sleeping in rearward lines or in works where they are allowed to take off their equipment, will sleep with their gas helmets round their necks, and must know exactly where their second helmet is to be found.

6. All gas helmets will be inspected at the commencement of every "ALERT" period in addition to the ordinary inspection.

7. R.A. sentries will be doubled.

8. An officer on duty will be detailed from each Company in reserve.

9. Gas helmets must always be worn outside the great coat.

10. Men will be forbidden to wear macintosh sheets round their shoulders, and will have the top button of their great coats undone.

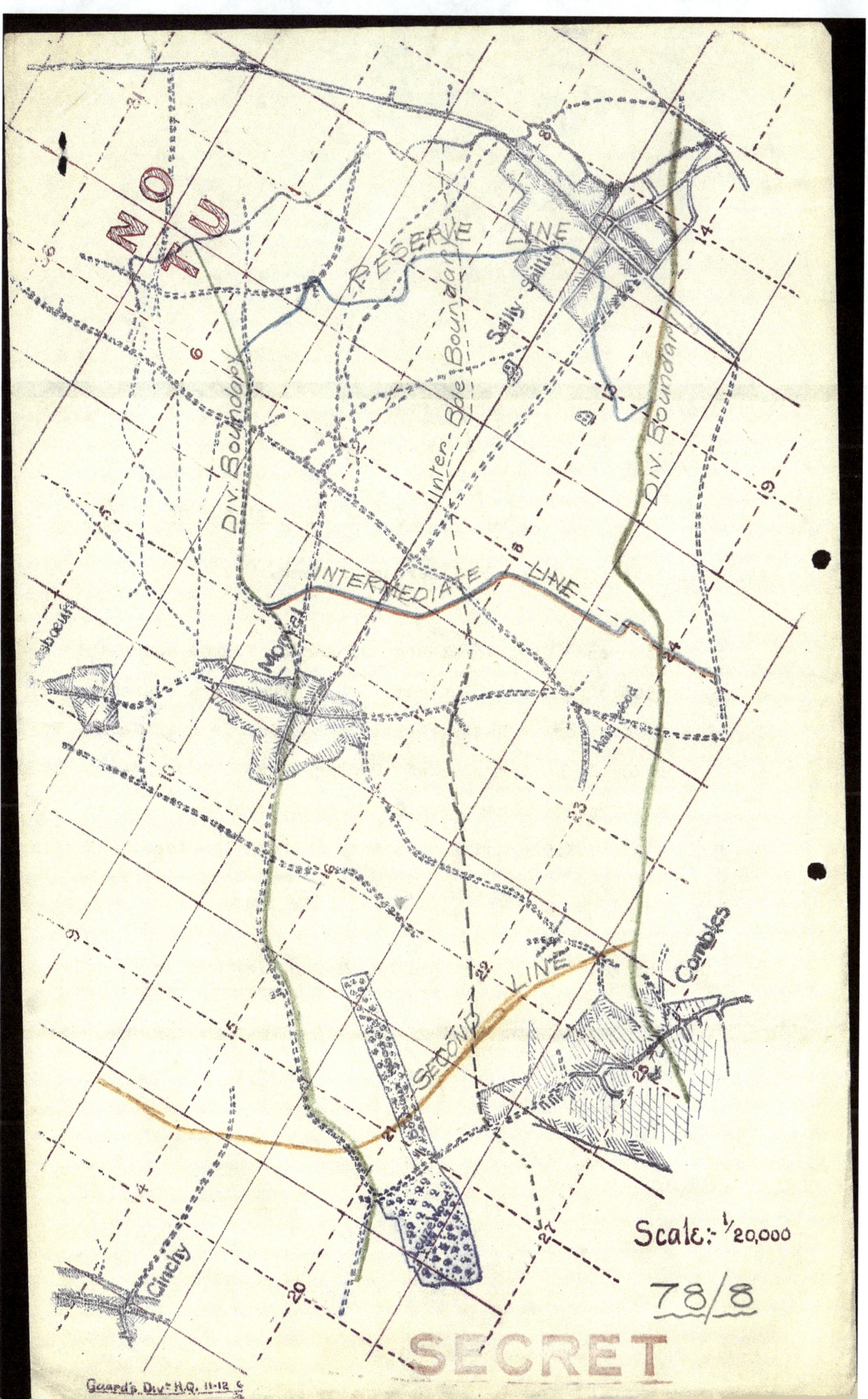

266

1st Guards Brigade No 805/1.

All recipients of Divl. Res. Defence Scheme.

 Reference Divisional Reserve Roster issued under this Office No 805 of the 15th instant. 1st Guards Brigade Machine Gun Coy. and Trench Mortar Battery relieve 2nd Guards Brigade M.G.Coy. and Trench Mortar Battery in left Sector on 18th instant.

 2nd Guards Brigade M.G.Coy. and T.M.Battery relieve 3rd Guards Bde M.G.Coy and T.M.Battery in Right Sector on 22nd inst.

                Captain.

16th Decr. 1916.   Brigade Major, 1st Guards Brigade.

SECRET.   (266)   1st G. B. No. 713.

1st Bn. Grenadier Guards.   2nd Guards Brigade.
2nd Bn. Grenadier Guards.   3rd Guards Brigade.
3rd Bn. Grenadier Guards.   1st Guards Brigade Machine Gun Coy.
4th Bn. Grenadier Guards.   2nd Guards Brigade Machine Gun Coy.
1st Bn. Coldstream Guards.   3rd Guards Brigade Machine Gun Coy.
2nd Bn. Coldstream Guards.   1st Guards Bde. T. M. Battery.
3rd Bn. Coldstream Guards.   2nd Guards Bde. T. M. Battery.
1st Bn. Scots Guards.   3rd Guards Bde. T. M. Battery.
2nd Bn. Scots Guards.   Guards Division.
1st Bn. Irish Guards.
2nd Bn. Irish Guards.
1st Bn. Welsh Guards.

Herewith Defence Scheme for Divisional Reserve.

This should be retained until the Division comes out of the line, or a new one is issued.

Please acknowledge receipt.

                                                     Captain.

3rd December 1916.   Brigade Major, 1st Guards Brigade.

SECRET.

Defence Scheme

for the Divisional Reserve of Guards Division.

Ref. Map = 57C S.W. 1/20,000.   December 3rd, 1916.

1.   The Divisional Reserve is under the Orders of the G.O.C., Guards Brigade in Reserve. H.Q., at present at SANDPITS Camp (E.24.b.)

COMPOSITION OF DIVNL. RESERVE.

2. (a) The Divisional Reserve is composed of the following troops :-

Bde., Machine Gun Company in Reserve.
Guards T. M. Battery in Reserve.
One Bn. Right Group at H Camp (after Dec.10th at BRONFAY FM.)
One Bn. Right Group at BRONFAY FARM.
One Bn. Left Group at BRONFAY FARM.
One Bn. Left Group at MEAULTE.

Units composing the Reserve are shown in attached table.

ACTION IN EVENT OF ATTACK.

3. (a) Reserve Brigade H.Q., will be prepared to move on receipt of Orders to ARROWHEAD Copse.

(b) Units will be prepared to move on receipt of Orders to MALTZHORN Camp (A.6.a. & b.) and O.C's Units are responsible that a sufficient number of Officers and N.C.O's per Company know the best route from their Camps to MALTZHORN Camp.

(c) Similarly, Units are responsible that a sufficient number of Officers and N.C.O's per Company know the best routes from MALTZHORN Camp to BOULEAUX Wood and the North Eastern edge of COMBLES.

(d) O.C., Bde. Machine Gun Company in Reserve will reconnoitre the Intermediate and 2nd Line with a view to being able to push forward Guns to reinforce these Lines of Defence, if so ordered.

INTERMEDIATE & 2ND LINES.

4. The Intermediate and 2nd Lines run as follows :-

<u>Intermediate Line.</u>   T.24.b.1.7 - T.18.d.0.0
                        T.18.a.5.0 - T.18.a.0.7
                        T.11.d.7.0 - T.11.d.0.7

<u>Second Line.</u>   T.29.a.1.8 - T.22.d.0.5
                        T.22.c.0.8 - T.21.central.

WARNING ORDER.

5. Should a Warning Order be issued instructing Units in Divnl. Reserve to stand by ready to move as in para. 3 above, the following will be proceeded with :-

(a) The filling of all water-bottles.
(b) The issuing of rations.
(c) The issuing of an extra bandolier of S.A.A. to each man.
(d) The issuing of all available Bombs.

                                                   Captain,
                   <u>Brigade Major, 1st Guards Brigade.</u>

BATTALIONS IN BACK AREA FORMING DIVISIONAL RESERVE.

	Left Group.			Right Group.	
DATE.	MEAULTE.	BRONFAY. 2.	BRONFAY. 1.	BRONFAY. 2.	H. CAMP.
Dec. 4.	1/G. G.	1/W. G.		2/G. G.	2/I. G.
Dec. 5.	1/G. G.	1/W. G.		2/G. G.	2/I. G.
Dec. 6.	1/G. G.	1/W. G.	3/G. G.		2/I. G.
Dec. 7.	1/G. G.	2/S. G.	3/G. G.		2/I. G.
Dec. 8.	1/G. G.	2/S. G.	3/G. G.		2/I. G.
Dec. 9.	3/G. G.	2/S. G.	2/G. G.		2/I. G.
Dec. 10.	3/G. G.	2/S. G.	2/G. G.	1/I. G.	

SECRET.   1st G. S. No. 715.

1st Bn. Grenadier Guards.   2nd Guards Brigade.
2nd Bn. Grenadier Guards.   3rd Guards Brigade.
3rd Bn. Grenadier Guards.   1st Guards Brigade Machine Gun Coy.
4th Bn. Grenadier Guards.   2nd Guards Brigade Machine Gun Coy.
1st Bn. Coldstream Guards.   3rd Guards Brigade Machine Gun Coy.
2nd Bn. Coldstream Guards.   1st Guards Bde. T. M. Battery.
3rd Bn. Coldstream Guards.   2nd Guards Bde. T. M. Battery.
1st Bn. Scots Guards.   3rd Guards Bde. T. M. Battery.
2nd Bn. Scots Guards.   Guards Division.
1st Bn. Irish Guards.
2nd Bn. Irish Guards.
1st Bn. Welsh Guards.

Herewith Defence Scheme for Divisional Reserve.

This should be retained until the Division comes out of the line, or a new one is issued.

Please acknowledge receipt.

                                                    J H Witts
                                                              Captain.
3rd December 1915.   Brigade Major, 1st Guards Brigade.

SECRET.

Defence Scheme

for the Divisional Reserve of Guards Division.

Ref. Map - GTC S.W. 1/10,000.   December 3rd, 1916.

1. The Divisional Reserve is under the Orders of the G.O.C.,
Guards Brigade in Reserve. H.Q., at present at MAIZIERES Camp
(V.14.d.)

COMPOSITION OF DIVISIONAL RESERVE.

2. (a) The Divisional Reserve is composed of the following troops :-

  Bde. Machine Gun Company in Reserve.
  Guards T.M. Battery in Reserve.
  One Bn. Right Group at R Camp (after Dec.10th at RUGBY Pk.)
  One Bn. Right Group at RUGBY Park.
  One Bn. Left Group at RUGBY Park.
  One Bn. Left Group at MEAULTE.

  Units composing the Reserve are shown in attached table.

ACTION IN EVENT OF ALARM.

3. (a) Reserve Brigade H.Q., will be prepared to move on receipt
of Orders to ARROWHEAD Copse.

  (b) Units will be prepared to move on receipt of Orders to
MAIZIERES Camp (O.I.A. & b.) and O.C's Units are responsible
that a sufficient number of Officers and N.C.O's per Company
know the best route from their Camps to MAIZIERES Camp.

  (c) Similarly, Units are responsible that a sufficient number
of Officers and N.C.O's per Company know the best routes from
MAIZIERES Camp to BOULEUX Wood and the North Eastern edge of
COMBLES.

  (d) O.C., Bde. Machine Gun Company in Reserve will reconnoitre
the Intermediate and 2nd Line with a view to being able to push
forward Guns to reinforce those Lines of Defence, if so ordered.

INTERMEDIATE & 2ND LINE.

4. The Intermediate and 2nd Lines run as follows :-

  Intermediate Line.   T.14.b.1.7 - T.15.d.0.0 -
                        T.15.d.5.0 - T.15.a.0.7 -
                        T.11.d.7.0 - T.11.d.0.7.

  Second Line.   T.10.a.1.5 - T.22.d.0.5 -
                        T.24.c.0.0 - T.21.central.

MARCHING ORDER.

5. Should a Warning Order be issued instructing Units in Dvnl.
Reserve to stand by ready to move as in para. 3 above, the
following will be proceeded with :-

  (a) The filling of all water-bottles.
  (b) The issuing of rations.
  (c) The issuing of an extra bandolier of S.A.A. to each man.
  (d) The issuing of all available Bombs.

J.H.Betts
Captain,
Brigade Major, 1st Guards Brigade.

SECRET.   Copy No.
----------   ----------

1st Guards Brigade Order No. 93.

Ref. Map - 57C S.W. 1/20,000.   16th December 1916.
----

1.   The following moves will take place tomorrow, December 17th :-

   (a)   The 2nd Bn. Irish Guards will arrange to move half the Company now in COMBLES to new shelters which have been dug about T 18 central. This move to be complete by 1 P.M.

   (b)   Sapping Platoon of 2nd Bn. Irish Guards will not move into the line with the Battn., but will move and occupy half the accommodation evacuated by the half Company moving up as detailed in para (a) above.

   (c)   The 3rd Guards Bde. T.M.Battery will move tomorrow from MALTZHORN Camp to T 28 b 9.5 (strong point). Move to be complete by 1 P.M.

         In the event of attack, 3rd Guards Bde. T.M.Battery will form part of the garrison of this strong point.

   (d)   The sapping Platoon of 2nd Bn. Grenadier Guards will on relief of their Battn., take over the accommodation evacuated by Sapping Platoon of 2nd Bn. Irish Guards.

2.   The Sapping Platoon of 3rd Bn. Coldstream Guards will on relief of their Battn., on 18th inst., move to COMBLES and take over the other half of the accommodation at T 28 b 3.3 which is being evacuated as detailed in para. 1 (a) above. The position of this accommodation should be reconnoitred in daylight.

3.   Until further Orders therefore the Battalion in the COMBLES Area will be disposed as follows :-

         Bn. H.Q. and 2 Coy's.   COMBLES Trench.
              1 Coy.   HAIE WOOD.
              1/2 Coy.   COMBLES T.28.b.3.3.
              1/2 Coy.   Intermediate Line T 18 Central.

4.   Sapping Platoons will not in future go into the line with their Battalions.

         ACKNOWLEDGE.

                                                       Captain,
                                   Brigade Major, 1st Guards Brigade.

Issued at 8-30 P.M.

Copy No. 1   2nd Bn. Grenadier Guards.
         2   2nd Bn. Coldstream Guards.
         3   3rd Bn. Coldstream Guards.
         4   1st Bn. Irish Guards.
         5   1st Bn. Coldstream Guards.
         6   2nd Bn. Irish Guards.
         7   2nd Guards Brigade.
         8   Guards Division.
         9   Camp Commandant, MALTZHORN.
        10   O.C., Signals.
        11   3rd Guards Bde. T.M.Battery.
        12)
        13) Retained.
        14

DAILY INTELLIGENCE REPORT
1ST GUARDS BRIGADE.

17th December 1916.

8 A.M. Dec. 16th to 8 A.M. to Dec. 17th.

OPERATIONS.

3rd Bn. Coldstream Guards relieved 1st Bn. Coldstream Guards as left Battalion.

HOSTILE ACTIVITY.

Front line - Very little rifle or machine gun fire.

Artillery - Fair number of shells on main of SAILLISEL and on our front trench at U 8 a 9.5.

Aircraft. - A few enemy aeroplanes over in the morning at moderate height.

Movement - At 6 A.M. 16th 2 Germans approached our trenches at U 14 b 5.8. They were fired at by Lewis Gun and made off.
At dusk 16th a German working party was seen at U 2 c 3.1 and was fired at with unknown result.

INTELLIGENCE.

Signs of fraternising were observed beyond our right flank during the 16th. Enemy attempted to walk about on top about U 8 c 7.2 but the right Company of Right Battn., fired at them and they retired.
A further report on this will follow.

Brigadier General,
Comndg., 1st Guards Brigade.

SECRET.   Copy No.

1st Guards Brigade Order No. 93.

Ref. Map - 57C S.W. 1/20,000.   16th December 1916.

1. The following moves will take place tomorrow, December 17th :-

    (a) The 2nd Bn. Irish Guards will arrange to move half the Company now in COMBLES to new shelters which have been dug about T 18 central. This move to be complete by 1 P.M.

    (b) Sapping Platoon of 2nd Bn. Irish Guards will not move into the line with the Battn., but will move and occupy half the accommodation evacuated by the half Company moving up as detailed in para (a) above.

    (c) The 3rd Guards Bde. T.M.Battery will move tomorrow from MALTZHORN Camp to T 28 b 9.5 (strong point). Move to be complete by 1 P.M.

    In the event of attack, 3rd Guards Bde. T.M.Battery will form part of the garrison of this strong point.

    (d) The sapping Platoon of 2nd Bn. Grenadier Guards will on relief of their Battn., take over the occommodation evacuated by Sapping Platoon of 2nd Bn. Irish Guards.

2. The Sapping Platoon of 3rd Bn. Coldstream Guards will on relief of their Battn., on 18th inst., move to COMBLES and take over the other half of the accommodation at T 28 b 3.3 which is being evacuated as detailed in para. 1 (a) above. The position of this accommodation should be reconnoitred in daylight.

3. Until further Orders therefore the Battalion in the COMBLES Area will be disposed as follows :-

    Bn. H.Q. and 2 Coy's.   COMBLES Trench.
    1 Coy.   HAIE WOOD.
    1/2 Coy.   COMBLES T.28.b.3.3.
    1/2 Coy.   Intermediate Line T 18 Central.

4. Sapping Platoons will not in future go into the line with their Battalions.

        ACKNOWLEDGE.

                                                Captain,
                                Brigade Major, 1st Guards Brigade.

Issued at 8-30 P.M.

Copy No.1   2nd Bn. Grenadier Guards.
       2   2nd Bn. Coldstream Guards.
       3   3rd Bn. Coldstream Guards.
       4   1st Bn. Irish Guards.
       5   1st Bn. Coldstream Guards.
       6   2nd Bn. Irish Guards.
       7   2nd Guards Brigade.
       8   Guards Division.
       9   Camp Commandant, MALTZHORN.
      10   O.C., Signals.
      11   3rd Guards Bde. T.M.Battery.
      12)
      13) Retained.
      14

TRENCH ROSTER.

Date	Left Front.	Right Front.	COMBLES Area.	MALTZHORN Camp.	Camp 108.	Camp 15.
Dec. 17th.	3/C.G.	2/G.G. out 2/I.G. in.	2/I.G. out 2/C.G. in.	1/C.G.	1/I.G.	2/C.G. out 2/G.G. in.
Dec. 18th.	3/C.G. out 2/C.G. in.	2/I.G.	2/C.G. out 1/I.G. in.	1/C.G.	1/I.G. out 3/C.G. in.	2/G.G.
" 19th.	2/C.G.	2/I.G. out 1/I.G. in.	1/I.G. out 1/C.G. in.	1/C.G. out 2/I.G. in.	3/C.G.	2/G.G.
" 20th.	2/C.G. out 1/C.G. in.	1/I.G.	1/C.G. out 2/G.G. in.	2/I.G.	3/C.G.	2/G.G. out 2/C.G. in.
" 21st.	1/C.G.	1/I.G. out 2/G.G. in.	2/G.G. out 3/C.G. in.	2/I.G.	3/C.G. out 1/I.G. in.	2/C.G.
" 22nd.	1/C.G. out 3/C.G. in.	2/G.G.	3/C.G. out 2/I.G. in.	2/I.G. out 1/C.G. in.	1/I.G.	2/G.G.
" 23rd.	3/C.G.	2/G.G. out 2/I.G. in.	2/I.G. out 2/C.G. in.	1/C.G.	1/G.G.	2/C.G. out 2/G.G. in.
" 24th.	3/C.G. out 2/C.G. in.	2/I.G.	2/C.G. out 1/I.G. in.	1/C.G.	1/G.G. out 3/C.G. in.	2/G.G.
" 25th.	2/C.G.	2/I.G. out 1/I.G. in.	1/I.G. out 1/C.G. in.	1/C.G. out 2/I.G. in.	3/C.G.	2/G.G.
" 26th.	2/C.G. out 1/C.G. in.	1/I.G.	1/C.G. out 2/G.G. in.	2/I.G.	3/C.G.	2/G.G. out 2/C.G. in.

S E C R E T.   1st G.B. No. 914.

```
2nd Grenadier Guards.        1st Gds.Bde.M.G.Company.
1st Coldstream Guards.       1st Gds.Bde.T.M.Battery.
2nd Coldstream Guards.       2nd Gds.Bde.M.G.Company.
3rd Coldstream Guards.       2nd Gds.Bde.T.M.Battery.
1st Irish Guards.            Bde. Supply Officer.
2nd Irish Guards.            Bde. Transport Officer.
Guards Division.             Camp Commandant - BRONFAY Camp.
2nd Guards Brigade.          Camp Commandant - MALTZHORN Camp.
3rd Guards Brigade.
12th Infantry Brigade.
```

Herewith continuation of Trench Roster for Right Guards Brigade Group.

A. KNOWLADGA

RELIEF ROSTER FOR RIGHT GROUP BATTN's.

Date.	Left front.	Right front.	COMBLES Area.	MALTZHORN Camp.	Camp 108.	Camp 15.
Dec. 26th.	2/C.G.out 1/C.G.in.	1/I.G.	1/C.G.out 2/G.G.in.	2/I.G.	3/C.G.	2/G.G.out 2/C.G.in.
27th.	1/C.G.	1/I.G. out 2/G.G.in.	2/G.G.out 3/C.G.in.	2/I.G.	3/C.G.out 1/I.G.in.	2/C.G.
28th.	1/C.G.out 3/C.G.in.	2/G.G.	3/C.G. out 2/I.G.in.	2/I.G.out 1/C.G.in.	1/I.G.	2/C.G.
29th.	3/C.G.	2/G.G.out 2/I.G.in.	2/I.G.out 2/G.G.in.	1/C.G.	1/I.G.	2/C.G.out 2/G.G.in.
30th.	3/C.G.out 2/C.G.in.	2/I.G.	2/C.G.out 1/I.G.in.	1/C.G.	1/I.G.out 3/C.G.in.	2/G.G.
31st.	2/C.G.	2/I.G.out 1/I.G.in.	1/I.G.out 1/C.G.in.	1/C.G.out 2/I.G.in.	3/C.G.	2/G.G.
Jan. 1st.	2/C.G.out 1/C.G.in.	1/I.G.	1/C.G.out.	2/I.G.	3/C.G.	2/G.G.out 2/C.G.in.
2nd.	1/C.G.	1/I.G.out.	-	2/I.G.	3/C.G.out 1/I.G.in.	2/G.G.
3rd.	1/C.G.out.					

30/12/1916.   Brigade Major, 1st Guards Brigade.

S E C R E T.
1st G.B. No.801/1.

2nd Bn. Grenadier Guards.	12th Infantry Brigade.
1st Bn. Coldstream Guards.	1st Gds.Bde. M.G.Company.
2nd Bn. Coldstream Guards.	2nd Gds.Bde. M.G.Company.
3rd Bn. Coldstream Guards.	3rd Gds.Bde. M.G.Company.
1st Bn. Irish Guards.	Right Group, G.D.A.
2nd Bn. Irish Guards.	75th Field Coy., R.E.
Guards Division.	1st Gds.Bde. Supply Officer.
2nd Guards Brigade.	2nd Gds.Bde. Supply Officer.
3rd Guards Brigade.	

Herewith an amended copy of 'Instructions No. 1 for Right Group' sent to you under this Office No. 801 of 15th inst., Please destroy the old copy and substitute the attached.

The Roster remains unaltered and a new one is therefore not attached.

<u>ACKNOWLEDGE</u>.

Captain,
Brigade Major, 1st Guards Brigade.

16th Decr. 1916.

Instruction No 1. for Right Group.

Subject - **RELIEF.**

1. Herewith amended Trench Roster from 17th inst., inclusive.

2. No troops of Battalions going into the line will pass BOIS de HAIE before 4 P.M.

3. (a) A Train for Battalions coming out of the line and moving to Camps 108 or 13 will leave TRONES Wood Siding for PLATEAU Siding at 3 A.M. on the night of their relief. The Train will be drawn up in the Station and troops may embark on arrival at the Siding.

   (b) A Soup Kitchen is being established at TRONES Wood Siding.

   (c) The horse ambulances will meet this Train to convey bad cases from the PLATEAU to Camp.

4. Battalions coming out of the line and moving to MALTZHORN Camp will move by march route.

5. A Train will leave PLATEAU Siding for TRONES Wood Siding at 1 P.M. on the day on which any Battalion has to move from Camps 13 or 108 to the COMBLES Area.

6. A Battalion moving into the COMBLES Area from MALTZHORN Camp will move by march route and will not move from Camp before 2 P.M.

7. All movement in and out of Camps or trenches will be by platoons in file at 100 yards interval. Troops, transport and pack animals must keep as far as possible to the right of the road.

8. Completion of all movements will be wired by means of XIV Corps Code "A" to Right Group H.Q., as soon as possible after movement is complete.

   Casualties or any difficulties occurring during the relief should be reported at the same time.

9. Billeting parties will always be sent in advance to take over Camps and Bivouacs.

10. Battalions moving into the line will always send in advance at least 1 N.C.O. per Company and per Battn., R.Q., to take over Stores, etc.,

11. Gum Boots will be drawn and handed back into Store as at present.

12. Battalions moving into the COMBLES Area will take up rations for that day and the following day. Rations for the 48 hours for which Battalions are in the line will be sent up by rail to COMBLES on the day on which Battalions move into the COMBLES Area. These rations will be met by Pack Animals and delivered to Battn., H.Q., in COMBLES under Brigade arrangements.

13. Within the next few days, Battalions will be made up to 200 Petrol Tins each, after which, Battalions will be responsible for their own supply of water in the trenches. No more Petrol Tins will be available.

14. The Soup Kitchen now on the HAIE WOOD Road will be moved to the LEUZE Wood Road within a few days.

Bde. Major, 1st Gds. Bde.

SECRET. 1st G.B. No.801/3.

2nd Bn. Grenadier Guards.	1st Guards Bde. M.G.Company.
1st Bn. Coldstream Guards.	2nd Guards Bde. M.G.Company.
2nd Bn. Coldstream Guards.	3rd Guards Bde. M.G.Company.
3rd Bn. Coldstream Guards.	1st Guards Bde. T.M.Battery.
1st Bn. Irish Guards.	2nd Guards Bde. T.M.Battery.
2nd Bn. Irish Guards.	3rd Guards Bde. T.M.Battery.
	2nd Guards Brigade (for information.)

INSTRUCTIONS NO. 3 FOR RIGHT GROUP.

Subject - RETURNS.

1. The following Returns will be rendered daily by the two Battalions in the front line :-

	Due Right Group H.Q.,
Morning report (by wire)	3-30 A.M.
Intelligence Report by orderly	10 A.M.
Evening report (by wire)	3-30 P.M.
Casualty report (by wire, covering period 12 noon to 12 noon.)	3-30 P.M.
Demand for R.E. Stores, etc.,	8-0 P.M.

2. The Machine Gun Company in the line will render an Intelligence report to reach these H.Q., at 10 A.M. daily; also a Casualty report - Nil returns to be rendered.

3. The Battalion and Trench Mortar Battery in COMBLES will also render a Casualty report - Nil return to be rendered.

4. Battalions in the Camps will only render Casualty returns if they have any casualties to report.

5. All Casualty reports will be addressed to Right Group H.Q., Casualties affecting Units of other Brigades will be reported to Brigades concerned.

6. The Intelligence report should be rendered under the following headinds :-

   1. Operations - (Patrols and Sniping.)
   2. Intelligence.
   3. Aircraft.
   4. Artillery.
   5. Work - Number of coils of wire put out to be stated.

   Map references should be given if possible. Approximate Map references are of great assistance but if they are only approximate, this fact should be stated.

   This report will cover the period from 8-30 A.M. to 8-30 A.M.

7. An outgoing Battalion must be careful to hand over the days Intelligence to the incoming Battalion.

8. Situation reports do not always show the true situation on the Battalion front and an effort should be made to make them of some real value as a Situation report.

9. The capture of a prisoner must be wired at once to Group H.Q., the Regiment to which the prisoner belongs being stated.

ACKNOWLEDGE.

17th December 1916.

Captain,
Brigade Major, 1st Guards Brigade.

SECRET.   1st G.B. No.801/4.

INSTRUCTIONS NO. 4 FOR RIGHT GROUP.

Subject – DEFENSIVE MEASURES.

AIRCRAFT.

1. At times lately the enemy's aircraft has been very active and impudent by flying very low and thus gaining valuable information.

    This low flying by hostile machines must be checked immediately by concentration of fire from every Machine Gun, Lewis Gun and rifle within reasonable range.

    Battalions must telephone through at once when a hostile machine appears and flies very low, so that one of our machines may be telephoned for. Group H.Q., are in direct communication with No. 9 Squadron, R.F.C.

PATROLLING.

2. Attention is drawn to the necessity for active patrolling, both in order to gain information concerning the state of the enemy's front line, his wire and his saps and to deny 'No Man's Land' to the enemy. The opportunity of taking a prisoner must never be missed as it is always of the utmost importance to keep in touch with the enemy's dispositions, in order to ascertain whether there is any concentration of troops on any part of the front.

    Patrols should be reminded of the advantage of a rifle over a bomb at any time, especially at night. Bombs should only be used or even carried by patrols under very exceptional circumstances.

    It should be the rule and not the exception for each Company to send out patrols every night.

OBSERVATION.

3. Observation posts should be constructed in each front line Battn., area.

    In order that full value may be got out of these observation posts, some means for rapid communication with the Artillery should be established.

DEFENCE SCHEMES.

4. At present no Defence Scheme has been issued by either of the Battn's. in the line or by the Support Battn., The Brigadier directs that a Scheme based on the Brigade Defence Scheme be issued at once by these Battn's. This Scheme must be in possession of all Company Commanders and if necessary, Subordinate Commanders.

    The importance of thinking out and having Orders issued to meet any eventuality cannot be too greatly impressed on all Commanders.

    A copy of these Defence Schemes will be sent to Group H.Q.,

19th December 1916.   Captain,
                              Brigade Major, 1st Guards Brigade.

2nd Grenadier Gds.,   3rd Coldstream Gds.,
1st Coldstream Gds., 1st Irish Gds.,
2nd Coldstream Gds., 2nd Irish Guards.

Daily Intelligence Report - 1st Guards Brigade.

8 A.M. Decr. 17th to 8 A.M. Decr. 18th.

OPERATIONS.

2nd Bn. Irish Guards relieved 2nd Bn. Grenadier Guards on right Battn., front. Relief complete by 7-25 P.M.

Patrols - A listening patrol went out from right Company, Left Battn., and got within 20 yards of enemy sap at U 8 b 2.6 - After waiting here it moved to near sap or angle of trench at U 8.b.3.0. There were no sounds of working at either of these places.

HOSTILE ACTIVITY.

Front Line - Enemy Machine Guns active during the night.

During afternoon of 17th opposite right Battn., a German shouted across in English "That they were Saxons and would not shoot unless we did". Should a German Officer come round they would fire high. It has been noticed that most of the bullets do go high.

Artillery - Between 4-30 P.M. and 5-30 P.M. 17th enemy heavily shelled ground in front of the QUARRY over which the outcoming relief was proceeding. Shells used 4.2" and 5.9" coming from direction of BUS. Otherwise enemy artillery less active than usual.

Aircraft - No enemy aircraft over during the day, probably owing to the foggy weather.

Movement - A relief probably took place opposite the whole Brigade Front. At 7-30 A.M. 18th the relieved Battn's.; were seen moving back opposite right Battn., front. Our Artillery then searched enemy tracks in rear of their line.

At 7-45 A.M. 18th enemy working party was seen taking duck-boards from a Dump at U 15 a 1.8 - They were dispersed by our Artillery.

INTELLIGENCE.

Signals - Enemy artillery fire at 4-30 P.M. on 17th followed the bursting of a Golden Rain rocket. Little observation possible on account of the foggy weather.

18/12/1916.

Lieut.,
Intelligence Officer, 1st Guards Bde.,

Daily Intelligence Report - 1st Guards Brigade.
----

8 A.M. Decr. 18th to 8 A.M. Decr. 19th.

OPERATIONS.

    Reliefs.   2nd Bn. Coldstream Guards relieved 3rd Bn. Coldstream Guards as left Battalion. Relief complete by 7-5 P.M.

    Patrol.   A patrol went out from right Company, Left Battalion - They confirmed the supposition that the reported sap at U 8 b 3.0 is only an angle of the main trench. It is 40 yards from our trench and there were no signs of work here.

HOSTILE ACTIVITY.

    Front Line.   Enemy very quiet except for sniping at night, particularly at where our communication trenches join the front line. At 6 P.M. 4 Germans were seen attending at their wire at U 8 a 8.9 and were dispersed by rifle fire. The enemy seem to be making a strong point in their front line at U 8 c 4.3 - A good deal of earth was thrown up here yesterday.
        Enemy patrol of 3 men seen at U 8 a 8.8 last night by a covering party.

    Artillery.   Activity below normal. Six shells 5.9" near SAILLY Church at 1-15 P.M.

    Trench Mortars.   Four small shells suspected to be Trench Mortar shells on main road SAILLY about 3-30 P.M.

    Aircraft.   No enemy aircraft.

MOVEMENT.

    At 9-30 A.M. 18th Company of enemy seen working in trench between O 32 c and O 32 d. Our Artillery shelled them and caused much confusion and probably casualties. Continual movement of small parties of men throughout the day near enemy second line at U 15 a 2.8. They were seen carrying trench boards, timber, hammers, sacks and filling sandbags. Men also seen moving about front line at U 14 b 9.7 with mud scoops - There seems to be a Dump at U 15 a 3.7 and our Artillery have registered on the spot.

    At 7-50 A.M. 18th, 20 Germans, possibly end of relief entered a trench at U 9 c 0.1.

    At 8-30 A.M. 18th a party was seen moving over the open about the same place and were shelled by our Artillery.

INTELLIGENCE.

    The area U 9 c and U 15 a is not visible from our front line but was observed by O.P. in Church at U 14 b 1.5 and also from support line. The area U 2 can be well observed from O.P. at U 8 c 5.8. These two O.P's are very valuable indeed.

    Locations.   A snipers post in sap at U 8 b 2.6. This is manned at night.

Signals.   A pink rocket from here brought a burst of Machine Gun fire from the main trench in rear.

At 1-5 A.M. two rockets (Green bursting into Golden Rain) went up from U 8 b 2.7.   No result.

White lights went up occasionally during the day beyond the Brigade left flank with no apparent result.

19th Decr. 1916.

Lieut.,
Intelligence Officer, 1st Guards Bde.,

Daily Intelligence Report. 1st Guards Bde.

8 a.m. Decr. 19th 1916 to 8 a.m. Decr. 20th 1916.

OPERATIONS.

    Reliefs. 1st Bn Irish Guards relieved 2nd Bn Irish Guards as Right Battalion. Relief complete by 7.15 p.m.

    Sniping. Snipers of right battalion accounted for two Germans.

    Patrols. No patrols went out.

HOSTILE ACTIVITY.

    Front line. Very little enemy activity. — A little sniping during the early part of the night. In front of right battalion enemy are reported to snipe at night-time from shell holes in front of our line. A machine fired from U 14 b 9.5.

    Artillery. Very quiet except for a few shells into COMBLES about 1.15 p.m. A few shells into SAILLY about 7.15 p.m. The troops on our right flank made a lot of noise relieving and got shelled as a result.

    Aircraft. No enemy aircraft seen.

INTELLIGENCE.

    Movement. From the O.P. in SAILLY CHURCH considerable movement was seen behind enemy front line at U 15 a 3.5. Owing to our sniping this movement diminished later. About 10 p.m. 19th a party of Germans was seen working on their parapet at U 14 b 8.5 and was fired at by a Lewis Gun. A Coldstream Guard Machine gunner lost his way about U 14 b 6.6 and got near the enemy line. He heard them coughing and returned without being fired at.

    Signals. During the early part of the night opposite the right battalion enemy sent up very lights from his reserve and support lines. Later on he only fired them from his front line. About 1 a.m. a golden rain rocket went up at U 14 b 8.4 no result apparent.

    Location. The enemy sap opposite the left battalion is at U 8 b 3.3 and not at U 8 b 2.6 as previously stated. The previous map reference of the right sap or angle of the trench at U 8 b 3.0 is probably correct.

    Miscellaneous. During the relief of troops on our right considerable shouting between the enemy and our troops appears to have occurred.

Lieut.
Intelligence Officer, 1st Guards Bde.

SECRET.   K.T.O.   1st G.B. No.801/6.

2nd Bn. Grenadier Guards.	3rd Bn. Coldstream Guards.
1st Bn. Coldstream Guards.	1st Bn. Irish Guards.
2nd Bn. Coldstream Guards.	2nd Bn. Irish Guards.

INSTRUCTIONS NO.6 FOR RIGHT GROUP.

Subject :- COMBLES Trench.

1. The accommodation in COMBLES Trench and in the shelters to the South, leaves much to be desired. Every effort will therefore be made by each Battalion to improve the accommodation.

2. A work party will be detailed every morning by the Battalion in COMBLES to work on the trench and on the shelters, under the supervision of an R.E. N.C.O.

3. Advanced parties of incoming Companies will reach Company H.Q., COMBLES Trench not later than 12-30 P.M. to take over -

    (a) the shelters available.
    (b) the scheme of work on improvements.
    (c) the tools and stores.
    (d) the Blankets.

4. Every effort will be made to collect the salvage lying round the trench: this will be taken to the Brigade Dump outside Brigade H.Q., in COMBLES.

5. The vicinity of the trench will be kept clean. Refuse and tins will be buried. Proper latrines will be built.

6. New material and salvaged material for improvements is available.

7. All unserviceable blankets will be collected and handed in to the Gum Boot Store in COMBLES where a receipt will be obtained.

    Care will be taken that blankets are kept dry and not trodden into the mud.

20th Decr. 1916.

Captain,
Brigade Major, 1st Guards Brigade.

Daily Intelligence Report, 1st Guards Brigade.

8 a.m. Decr. 20th 1916 – 8 a.m. 21st Decr. 1916.

OPERATIONS.

Reliefs. 1st Bn Coldstream Guards relieved 2nd Bn Coldstream Guards as left Battalion. Relief complete by 7.30 p.m.

Patrols. Left Battalion sent out a patrol from U 8 a 9.5. No enemy patrols seen but the enemy were heard tapping in pickets in their trench about U 8 b 1.8.
Right Battalion sent out a patrol from the gap at U 14 b 7.5. No enemy patrols seen. The enemy trench opposite was heavily wired and the enemy were heard knocking in stakes in their trench.

HOSTILE ACTIVITY.

Front line.
Enemy sniping opposite Right Battalion has increased considerably – otherwise enemy was fairly quiet and there was very little machine gun fire.
Three rifle grenades were fired at our support line at U 14 b 4.6.

Artillery.
About 11.15 a.m. our support line at U 14 b 4.6 was shelled by 4.2" and 77 m.m. guns. Also the support trench of left battalion at U 8 c 8.8 and the valley at U 7 d 9.5 otherwise less activity than usually.

AIRCRAFT. Enemy aircraft fairly active between 9.30 and 12 noon. One Aeroplane flew very low over our lines and our machine gun fire seemed to have no effect. Between 3.30 p.m. and dusk two enemy aeroplanes over our line. Before turning back they dropped a single bright white light – no effect.
An aeroplane was brought down in flames near ROCQUIGNY. Nationality unknown.

INTELLIGENCE.

Movement. East of ROCQUIGNY a train was seen about O 28 d.
Enemy worked at angle of trench at U 8 d 4.1 early on morning of 20th.
Enemy worked all day (20th) on their trench at U 14 b 9.8 and a good deal of hammering at night is heard at this point. A good deal of earth thrown up at U 9 c 0.0 and early on morning of 20th a carrying party of 25 Germans entered a trench here. They seem to have made a dump here and may possibly be making a communication trench from support to 1st line at this point.

Identifications.
Several enemy seen in ruins of SAILLISEL – one man with a white cap band and the rest with red cap bands.

Miscellaneous.
Beyond our right, Germans and British, including Officers are reported to walk about "No Man's Land" and collect wood. They do not appear to speak to one another or to fraternise in any way.
From trench at U 14 b 9.7 enemy red cross men made signs that they wished to come and bury a dead German lying in "No Man's Land". They were warned not to do so and did not leave their trench.

Lieut.
Intelligence Officer, 1st Guards Bde.

SECRET.　　　　　　　　　　　　　　　　　　　　　1st G.B. No. 15

(279) 1st Guards Brigade Order No. 94.

21st December 1916.

1.   On the night of Decr. 22nd/23rd, 2nd Guards Bde. M.G.Company and T.M.Battery will relieve 3rd Guards Bde. M.G.Company and T.M.Battery in the right Sector.

2.   No troops or transport of 2nd Guards Bde. M.G.Company to pass the East edge of COMBLES before 6 P.M.

3.   Train up from PLATEAU is available at 1 P.M. on Decr. 22nd and down from TRONES Wood Siding at 3 A.M. on 23rd for troops of these Units.

4.   Completion of relief to be reported by Code "A".

ACKNOWLEDGE.

Captain,
Brigade Major, 1st Guards Brigade.

Copy No. 1 2nd Gds.Bde.M.G.Coy.　　No. 8 3rd Coldstream Gds.,
      2 2nd Gds.Bde.T.M.Bty.　　 9 1st Irish Gds.,
      3 3rd Gds.Bde.M.G.Coy.　　 10 2nd Irish Gds.,
      4 3rd Gds.Bde.T.M.Bty.　　 11 Guards Division.
      5 2nd Grenadier Gds.,　　 12 2nd Guards Brigade.
      6 1st Coldstream Gds.,　　 13 3rd Guards Brigade.
      7 2nd Coldstream Gds.,　　 14 O.C., Signals.
          15 & 16 Retained.

SECRET.　　　　　　　　　　　　　　　　　　　　1st G.B. No.

1st Guards Brigade Order No. 94.

21st December 1916.

1. On the night of Decr. 22nd/23rd, 2nd Guards Bde. M.G.Company and T.M.Battery will relieve 3rd Guards Bde. M.G.Company and T.M.Battery in the right Sector.

2. No troops or transport of 2nd Guards Bde. M.G.Company to pass the East edge of COMBLES before 6 P.M.

3. Train up from PLATEAU is available at 1 P.M. on Decr. 22nd and down from TRONES Wood Siding at 3 A.M. on 23rd for troops of these Units.

4. Completion of relief to be reported by Code "A".

ACKNOWLEDGE.

Captain,
Brigade Major, 1st Guards Brigade.

```
Copy No. 1  2nd Gds.Bde.M.G.Coy.    No. 8  3rd Coldstream Gds.,
         2  2nd Gds.Bde.T.M.Bty.        9  1st Irish Gds.,
         3  3rd Gds.Bde.M.G.Coy.       10  2nd Irish Gds.,
         4  3rd Gds.Bde.T.M.Bty.       11  Guards Division.
         5  2nd Grenadier Gds.,        12  2nd Guards Brigade.
         6  1st Coldstream Gds.,       13  3rd Guards Brigade.
         7  2nd Coldstream Gds.,       14  O.C., Signals.
                    15 & 16 Retained.
```

Daily Intelligence Report, 1st Guards Brigade.
----

8 a.m. Decr. 21st 1916 to 8 a.m. Decr. 22nd 1916.

OPERATIONS.

Relief. 2nd Bn Grenadier Guards relieved 1st Bn Irish Guards as right battalion. Relief complete by 6.49 p.m.

Patrols. A patrol of left battalion went out from U 8 b 1.4 it went up to enemy wire at U 8 b 0.7 - The enemy trench here appeared lightly held and baling of water was going on. The wire here appeared rather thick. "No Man's Land" here is much cut up by shell fire. The right battalion sent out a patrol which visited trench about U 8 b 3.4. This is probably used for listening purposes as a working party had been observed earlier.
Another patrol lay near enemy trench at U 8 d 5.2 but neither saw nor heard enemy.

Sniping. Snipers fired down the BAPAUME Road at dusk from U 8 b 1.5.

HOSTILE ACTIVITY.

Front line.
Very little sniping or machine gun fire. A German looked over his trench and waved from about U 2 c 5.1 as though trying to fraternise. He was fired at with unknown result.
Enemy working all day at cleaning trench at U 14 b 9.8 The trench appears to be deep and has no wire in front of it.

Artillery.
Slightly more active opposite right battalion. 4.2" shells at U 14 b 3.6 and shrapnel over the Quarry during the day. A few shells on support line (U 8 c 8.8) and reserve line (U 13 a 8.8) of left battalion also at U 14 b 3.6 about midnight.

Trench Mortars.
Our machine gunners say an aerial torpedo fell in SAILLY at 11 p.m. Further confirmation needed.

Aircraft.
Very active during the morning of 21st.

INTELLIGENCE.

Movement.
Two trains seen going eastwards to the North of BUS. - A siding is suspected here. Small parties of enemy moving about in U 3 - Small parties carried sandbags from ROCQUIGNY up to points on ROCQUIGNY - SAILLISEL road about U 3 a.
The wire South and South-West of ROCQUIGNY appears strong, also along east side of road at O 33 b 1.6

Signals. Red and green lights went up from enemy lines occasionally without any apparent result. Purple lights from U 14 b 9.9 were answered by purple lights about U 10.

Location.
A machine gun emplacement at U 8 b 3.4.

Lieut.
Intelligence Officer, 1st Guards Brigade.

Daily Intelligence Report, 1st Guards Brigade.
----

8 a.m. 22nd Decr. 1916 to 8 a.m. Decr. 23rd 1916.

OPERATIONS.
- Reliefs. 3rd Bn Coldstream Guards relieved 1st Bn Coldstream Guards as left battalion. Relief complete at 7 p.m.
  2nd Bde M.G. Coy relieved 3rd Bde M.G. Coy.
- Patrols. Patrols from Right battalion reconnoitred supposed enemy Sap at U 14 b 8.9 - No sounds or signs of enemy - Support Coy. of right battalion located support and reserve lines of Brigade on our right.
- Locations. Support line of Brigade on our right - runs South from U 14 b 4.1. Reserve line. Extreme left on the BAPAUME Road at U 14 c 1.4.
- Artillery. Our Artillery shelled the Mound U 2 c 9.1 at 12.30 p.m.

HOSTILE ACTIVITY.
- Front line. Except for a little sniping from U 8 d 3.4, enemy were very quiet. Much work especially baling water seemed to be going on in enemy front line. At 4 p.m. an explosion throwing up columns of water and earth took place in enemy front trench at U 14 b 8.9 At 12.45 p.m. 2 Germans left their trench about 14 b 10.5 as if coming over to surrender, but bolted back and although fired at were not hit.
- Artillery. Intermittent Field Gun shelling near SAILLY CHURCH during the day - About 11 a.m. a few 5.9" shells near the BAPAUME Road at U 8 c.
- Aircraft. Three German aeroplanes high over our lines at 4 p.m.

INTELLIGENCE.
- Movements. U 9 c 5.5.
  6 enemy seen approaching across the open at U 14 b 9.9 They were unarmed and were probably a relief for a M.G. post at U 14 b 9.9.
  There is a dump of duckboards at O 32 c 4.2. A good deal of movement in LE MESNIL. 4 horsemen were seen in front of the village, and two trains came up to it from East at 3.30 p.m. and 3.50 p.m.
  Horse traffic noticed on the LE MESNIL - ROCQUIGNY Road and a train of 30 trucks moving from BUS to BARASTRE.
- Signals. Artillery to lengthen range - Purple lights, also a green spray rocket. Yesterday evening Germans sent up many green lights without any result being apparent.

JACL

Lieut.
Intelligence Officer, 1st Guards Brigade.

SECRET.   1st G.B. No.922.

DEFENCE SCHEME
RIGHT GUARDS BRIGADE GROUP.

281/A

BOUNDARIES.

1.   The front to be held by the Brigade extends from about
U.14.b.7.6. to U.8.a.5.7.

   Southern Boundary -
   U.14.b.7.6. - U.14.a.3.0. - U.13.d.0.5. -
   T.18.d.5.0. - T.24.b.0.2. - T.23.d.0.2. -
   T.29.b.4.0.

   Northern Boundary -
   U.8.a.5.7. - U.7.b.2.0. - U.7.c.0.2. -
   T.12.d.3.1. - T.18.a.0.0. - T.23.a.0.9. -
   T.22.c.0.5.

   Inter Battn. Boundary -
   U.8.c.9.3. - U.8.c.0.0. - U.13.b.1.6.

ORGANIZATION OF DEFENCE.

2.   The defensive system will be organised as follows :-

   (a)   Front line system of fire and support trenches.

   (b)   A reserve trench on an average of 500 yards behind the
front line - i.e. the present reserve trench held by 1
Company of the left Battn, which will eventually be extended
to the Chapel of SAILLY CHATEAU - thence it will turn back
through the CHATEAU Strong Point and thence along the line
of the Southern duck-boards (CHATEAU Avenue) to U.13.c.9.8.
where it will join the reserve line of the Brigade on our
right.

   (c)   A switch line consisting of strong points on the general
line SAILLY-SAILLISEL CHURCH - U.13.Central - HAIE WOOD for
the protection of the Right Flank of the Division.
Strong points have been constructed at the following places :-
U.14.b.2.4.(SALLY Point). U.13.b.5.5.(GOPSE Point).
U.28.b.9.5.(COMBLES Point). A new strong point is about
to be constructed at U.14.a.5.3.(CUSHY Point).

   (d)   The intermediate line running from about T.18.a.3.3.
through T.18.Central to T.24.Central. This line has actually
been dug on the ground to a depth of about 2 ft.

   (e)   The second line running from T.22.b.0.8. to T.29.a.0.9.
(not yet dug).

   (f)   Defended localities at the N.E. extremity of COMBLES and
at LEUZE Wood (not yet constructed).

DISTRIBUTION OF INFANTRY.

3. Right Guards Brigade Group Headquarters - COMBLES CATACOMBS.

Right Sub-sector - 2 Companies front line.
1 Company Support line.
1 Company QUARRY, U.13.a.3.5.
Battn. H.Q., QUARRY, U.13.a.3.5.

Left Sub-sector - 2 Companies front line.
1 Company Support line.
1 Company in Reserve line about U.7.d.central.

Support Battn. - Battn., H.Q., COMBLES.
2 Companies COMBLES Trench, T.27.b.
1 Company HAIE Wood, T.23.b.
1 Company Intermediate line.

In the event of attack this Battn., will be prepared to move, on receipt of orders, any Company to the following places :-

(i) To man CHATEAU Avenue (the old communication trench which runs from MOUCHOIR COPSE to SAILLY CHATEAU).
(ii) To move to the Intermediate line.
(iii) To move to the CHATEAU or COPSE Strong Points - the QUARRY - or Reserve Line.

Reserve Battn. - MALTZHORN Camp.

In the event of attack this Battn., will be prepared to move, on receipt of orders, to the 2nd Line or any of the places mentioned for the Support Battn., above. It is essential that every Company and Platoon Commander of Support and Reserve Battn's. knows the best routes under cover from view to all these places.

ARTILLERY SUPPORT.

4. (a) Right Group Guards Divnl. Artillery supports the Brigade Group. Right Group Artillery H.Q., are at T.28.c.7$\frac{1}{2}$.3.

(b) Each Battn., in the line will be connected by telephone direct with a Battery.

(c) By night an Artillery Liaison Officer will remain at Battn., H.Q., of Battn's, in the line.

(d) From dawn to dusk the Liaison Officer will be observing from some point in each front line Battn., Area. He is responsible that his position is known to Battn., and Company Commanders.

(e) Infantry O.P's must ascertain every morning from Battn. H.Q., the position of the Liaison Officer, so that Artillery can immediately be turned on to any target that the enemy presents.

MACHINE GUNS

MACHINE GUNS.

5.   There are 8 Machine Guns in the front line. Company and Platoon Commanders in whose Area these Guns are placed must not only know their positions but also the ground which they would sweep in the event of an attack. Lewis Guns can then be placed so as to supplement the fire of these Machine Gun's at the most important points or to cover ground which in the event of an attack would not be swept by Machine Gun fire.

Other Machine Gun's in the Area are situated as follows :-

2 Guns in Reserve line about T.7.d.central.
1 Gun in QUARRY U.13.a.3.5.
2 Guns in Intermediate Line T.18.c.
2 Guns in COMBLES Strong Point T.28.b.9.5.

In the event of attack the remaining Gun of the Machine Gun Company will be moved to CHATEAU Strong Point.

R.E.

6.   (a)   The 75th Field Coy., R.E. H.Q., are in COMBLES Catacombs. In the event of attack they will 'stand to' in billets.

(b)   Sapping Platoons will act in a similar manner to the R.E.

CARRYING PARTIES ETC.,

7.   In the event of an attack while any Unit not composing the normal garrison is employed in the front line Area, the Officer or N.C.O. in charge of the party will immediately report to the nearest Battn., or Company Commander for Orders.

GAS ATTACK.

8.   In case of a "GAS ATTACK", the alarm will be spread by every means available.

Telephone Operators will send "GAS" to all concerned. Infantry, Lewis Guns and Machine Guns will open a steady regulated fire on the German Trenches.

Artillery will open a deliberate fire on the German Trenches and get ready for rapid barrage in case of receipt of "S.O.S" message, or on seeing the "S.O.S" Rocket Signal.

NOTE.   In spreading the alarm for Gas Shell Bombardments, Strombus Horns, Gongs, and other Signals for a Gas Attack will not be employed.

"S.O.S."

9.   The "S.O.S" telephone message or "S.O.S" Rocket Signal, means that the Germans are actually leaving their trenches to attack, and that rapid barrage is required from Guns and from Machine Guns that can barrage in front of our front line.

The/

The "S.O.S" Signal for XIV Corps is one green — one white rocket — fired in rapid succession and repeated until acted upon by the Artillery.

signature
Captain,
Brigade Major, 1st Guards Brigade.

23rd December 1916.

SECRET.

1st G.B. No. 922.

2nd Grenadier Guards.   2nd Gds. Bde. T.M. Btty.,
1st Coldstream Guards.   Guards Division.
2nd Coldstream Guards.   2nd Guards Brigade.
3rd Coldstream Guards.   3rd Guards Brigade.
1st Irish Guards.   12th Infantry Brigade.
2nd Irish Guards.   75th Field Coy., R.E.
2nd Gds. Bde. M.G. Coy.,   Right Group, G.D.A.,

Herewith DEFENCE SCHEME of Right Guards Brigade Group.

Please destroy the Provisional Scheme issued under 2/G.B.305/G.

ACKNOWLEDGE.

signature
Captain,
Brigade Major, 1st Guards Brigade.

23rd December 1916.

APPENDIX "A".

PRINCIPLES OF DEFENCE.

The following principles will be adopted in holding the line :-

(a)   The front line will be held as thinly as is consistent with security. To permit of thus holding the front line, good wire entanglements are necessary, good arrangements for flank defence, and close and continuous observation on the part of Artillery F.O.O's.

(b)   Troops will NOT fall back from one line to any other line, but all ground will be defended as long as possible whether the flanks are turned or not.

(c)   There are three kinds of attack which may be anticipated:-

   (i)   A raid.

   (ii) An attack on a minor scale to capture some locality, accompanied by a bombardment.

   (iii) A serious attack preceded by a heavy bombardment.

(d)   As regards (c) (i) :-

   Vigilance, active patrolling, combined with a good system of listening posts and wire, make the failure of such attacks certain.

(e)   As regards (c) (ii) :-

   Should the enemy succeed in establishing himself in our trenches, he should be counter attacked immediately from both flanks and from the support trenches where available in sufficiently close proximity.

   The extent and intensity of the enemy's bombardment if closely observed should give an indication of his objective and enable preparations for counter attack to be made before his attack is delivered. The essential is to deny him time in which to consolidate.

   Should the counter attack fail, the captured portion of our trenches must be isolated by blocking, and support trenches firmly held until more deliberate preparations can be made.

   Meanwhile, the Artillery will prevent enemy reinforcements crossing "No Man's Land", and the Infantry must do their utmost to reconnoitre and locate the exact position held by the enemy, so that our Artillery may bombard the captured trenches with precision: thus further counter attack by our reserves will be executed under the most favourable conditions.

   Artillery/

Artillery fire will be opened on the captured trenches without the sanction of the Guards Brigadier concerned.

(f) **As regards (a) (iii) :-**

It is unlikely that such an attack will come as a surprise, and Commanders will have time to make suitable dispositions.

In any case, no good will be gained by reinforcing the front line.

Supporting troops must hold their ground, and by means of fire and local attacks keep the enemy in check until sufficient reserves are available to assume the offensive.

(g) All Officers must consider the action to be taken by the troops under their command in the event of attack on any portion of the front for the defence of which they are responsible. Plans must be thought out beforehand, and the action to be taken known to all. Nothing should be left to chance.

Battalions and Companies must keep each other informed of their plans to meet various eventualities.

Officers Commanding Battalions in the line will always issue a Defence Scheme to their Company Commanders. This Defence Scheme should be handed over from Battn., to Battn., on relief. It should not contain any information concerning dispositions other than those of the Battn., concerned. A copy will always be sent to Brigade H.Q.,

The action to be taken by Support and Reserve Coy's. in the event of an attack should always be clearly stated, also any special tasks or special points to be defended by Lewis Guns. The action of Reserve Lewis Guns will also be laid down.

It should also be made clear that O.C., Reserve Coy's. must know the position of Units on their right and left, even though they belong to another Division or Brigade.

APPENDIX "B".

GAS ALERT.

When the wind is between N.W. and S.E. Guards Brigades in the line will send the message "ALERT" to all Units under their Command, also to supporting Artillery Group and other attached Units.

The extra precautions to be taken on receipt of this message are as follows :-

EXTRA PRECAUTIONS TO BE TAKEN DURING A GAS ATTACK.

1. All men in positions where they are liable to be suddenly overwhelmed by gas will wear their helmets rolled up and pinned on front of the coat (as per instructions G.D. 1566/G.)

2. A sentry will be posted on every tunnel dugout, or other dugout holding more than 10 men.

3. A sentry will be posted on each group of two or three small dugouts.

4. A sentry will be posted on each Hd.Qrs. and Signal Office.

5. Men sleeping in rearward lines or in works where they are allowed to take off their equipment will sleep with their gas helmets round their necks, and must know exactly where their second helmet is to be found.

6. All gas helmets will be inspected at the commencement of every "ALERT" period in addition to the ordinary inspection.

7. R.A. sentries will be doubled.

8. An officer on duty will be detailed from each Company in Reserve.

9. Gas helmets must always be worn outside the greatcoat.

10. Men will be forbidden to wear macintosh sheets round their shoulders, and will have the top button of their greatcoats undone.

SECRET.   1st G.B. No. 022.

2nd Grenadier Guards.   2nd Gds. Bde. T.M. Btty.,
1st Coldstream Guards.   Guards Division.
2nd Coldstream Guards.   2nd Guards Brigade.
3rd Coldstream Guards.   3rd Guards Brigade.
1st Irish Guards.   12th Infantry Brigade.
2nd Irish Guards.   75th Field Coy., R.E.
2nd Gds. Bde. M.G. Coy.,   Right Group, G.D.A.,

Herewith DEFENCE SCHEME of Right Guards Brigade Group.

Please destroy the Provisional Scheme issued under 2/G.B.305/G.

ACKNOWLEDGE.

                                                           Captain,
23rd December 1915.   Brigade Major, 1st Guards Brigade.

SECRET.   1st G.B. No.???.

DEFENCE SCHEME
RIGHT GUARDS BRIGADE GROUP.

BOUNDARIES.

1. The front to be held by the Brigade extends from about U.14.b.7.6. to U.8.a.5.7.

   Southern Boundary -
   U.14.b.7.6. - U.14.a.3.0. - U.13.d.0.5. -
   T.18.d.5.0. - T.24.b.0.2. - T.23.d.0.2. -
   T.28.b.4.0.

   Northern Boundary -
   U.8.a.5.7. - U.7.b.2.0. - U.7.c.0.2. -
   T.12.d.3.1. - T.18.a.0.0. - T.23.a.0.9. -
   T.22.c.0.5.

   Inter Battn. Boundary -
   U.8.c.9.3. - U.8.c.0.0. - U.13.b.1.6.

ORGANIZATION OF DEFENCE.

2. The defensive system will be organised as follows :-

   (a) Front line system of fire and support trenches.

   (b) A reserve trench on an average of 500 yards behind the front line - i.e. the present reserve trench held by 1 Company of the left Battn. which will eventually be extended to the Chapel of SAILLY CHATEAU - thence it will turn back through the CHATEAU Strong Point and thence along the line of the Southern duck-boards (CHATEAU Avenue) to U.13.c.9.0. where it will join the reserve line of the Brigade on our right.

   (c) A switch line consisting of strong points on the general line SAILLY-SAILLISEL CHURCH - U.13. Central - HAIE WOOD for the protection of the Right Flank of the Division. Strong points have been constructed at the following places :-
   U.14.b.2.4. (SALLY Point). U.13.b.5.5. (COPSE Point).
   U.29.b.9.5. (COMBLES Point). A new strong point is about to be constructed at U.14.a.5.3. (CUSHY Point).

   (d) The intermediate line running from about T.18.a.3.3. through T.18.Central to T.24.Central. This line has actually been dug on the ground to a depth of about 2 ft.

   (e) The second line running from T.33.c.8. to T.29.a.0.9. (not yet dug).

   (f) Defended localities at the N.E. extremity of COMBLES and at LEUZE Wood (not yet constructed).

DISTRIBUTION OF INFANTRY.

3.   Right Guards Brigade Group Headquarters - COMBLES CATACOMBS.

Right Sub-sector - 2 Companies front line.
1 Company Support line.
1 Company QUARRY, U.13.a.3.5.
Battn. H.Q., QUARRY, U.13.c.3.5.

Left Sub-sector - 2 Companies front line.
1 Company Support line.
1 Company in Reserve line about U.7.d.central.

Support Battn., - Battn. H.Q., COMBLES.
2 Companies COMBLES Trench, T.27.b.
1 Company MALE Wood, T.33.b.
1 Company Intermediate line.

In the event of attack this Battn., will be prepared to move, on receipt of orders, any Company to the following places :-

(i)   To man CHATEAU Avenue (the old communication trench which runs from MOUCHOIR COPSE to SAILLY CHATEAU).
(ii) To move to the Intermediate Line.
(iii) To move to the CHATEAU or COPSE Strong Points - the QUARRY - or Reserve Line.

Reserve Battn., - HALTZHORN Camp.

In the event of attack this Battn., will be prepared to move, on receipt of orders, to the 2nd Line or any of the places mentioned for the Support Battn., above. It is essential that every Company and Platoon Commander of Support and Reserve Battn's., knows the best routes under cover from view to all these places.

ARTILLERY SUPPORT.

4. (a)   Right Group Guards Divnl. Artillery supports the Brigade Group. Right Group Artillery H.Q., are at T.38.c.7$\frac{1}{2}$.3

(b)   Each Battn. in the line will be connected by telephone direct with a Battery.

(c)   By night an Artillery Liaison Officer will remain at Battn., H.Q., of Battn's. in the line.

(d)   From dawn to dusk the Liaison Officer will be observing from some point in each front line Battn. Area. He is responsible that his position is known to Battn. and Company Commanders.

(e)   Infantry O.P's must ascertain every morning from Battn. H.Q., the position of the Liaison Officer, so that Artillery can immediately be turned on to any target that the enemy presents.

MACHINE GUNS

MACHINE GUNS.

5. There are 8 Machine Guns in the front line. Company and Platoon Commanders in whose Area these Guns are placed must not only know their positions but also the ground which they would sweep in the event of an attack. Lewis Guns can then be placed so as to supplement the fire of these Machine Gun's at the most important points or to cover ground which in the event of an attack would not be swept by Machine Gun fire.

Other Machine Gun's in the Area are situated as follows :-

2 Guns in Reserve line about T.7.d.central.
1 Gun in QUARRY U.13.a.3.5.
2 Guns in Intermediate Line T.18.c.
2 Guns in COMBLES Strong Point T.28.b.9.5.

In the event of attack the remaining Gun of the Machine Gun Company will be moved to CHATEAU Strong Point.

R.E.

6. (a) The 75th Field Coy., R.E. H.Q., are in COMBLES Catacombs. In the event of attack they will stand to in billets.

(b) Sapping Platoons will act in a similar manner to the R.E.

CARRYING PARTIES ETC.

7. In the event of an attack while any Unit not composing the normal garrison is employed in the front line Area, the Officer or N.C.O. in charge of the party will immediately report to the nearest Battn., or Company Commander for Orders.

GAS ATTACK.

8. In case of a "GAS ATTACK", the alarm will be spread by every means available.

Telephone Operators will send "GAS" to all concerned. Infantry, Lewis Guns and Machine Guns will open a steady regulated fire on the German Trenches.

Artillery will open a deliberate fire on the German Trenches and get ready for rapid barrage in case of receipt of "S.O.S" message, or on seeing the "S.O.S" Rocket Signal.

NOTE. In spreading the alarm for Gas Shell Bombardments, Strombus Horns, Gongs, and other Signals for a Gas Attack will not be employed.

"S.O.S."

9. The "S.O.S" telephone message or "S.O.S" Rocket Signal, means that the Germans are actually leaving their trenches to attack, and that rapid barrage is required from Guns and from Machine Guns that can barrage in front of our front line.

The/

- 4 -

The "S.O.S" Signal for XIV Corps is one ~~white~~ [green] - one ~~green~~ [white] - one ~~white~~ [green] rocket - fired in rapid succession and repeated until acted upon by the Artillery.

M. Smith

Captain,

23rd December 1916.   Brigade Major, 1st Guards Brigade.

APPENDIX "A".

PRINCIPLES OF DEFENCE.

The following principles will be adopted in holding the line :-

(a) The front line will be held as thinly as is consistent with security. To permit of thus holding the front line, good wire entanglements are necessary, good arrangements for flank defence, and close and continuous observation on the part of Artillery F.O.O's.

(b) Troops will NOT fall back from one line to any other line, but all ground will be defended as long as possible whether the flanks are turned or not.

(c) There are three kinds of attack which may be anticipated:-

(i) A raid.

(ii) An attack on a minor scale to capture some locality, accompanied by a bombardment.

(iii) A serious attack preceded by a heavy bombardment.

(d) <u>As regards (c) (i)</u> :-

Vigilance, active patrolling, combined with a good system of listening posts and wire, make the failure of such attacks certain.

(e) <u>As regards (c) (ii)</u> :-

Should the enemy succeed in establishing himself in our trenches, he should be counter attacked immediately from both flanks and from the support trenches where such are in sufficiently close proximity.

The extent and intensity of the enemy's bombardment if closely observed should give an indication of his objective and enable preparations for counter attack to be made before his attack is delivered. The essential is to deny him time in which to consolidate.

Should the counter attack fail, the captured portion of our trenches must be isolated by blocking, and support trenches firmly held until more deliberate preparations can be made.

Meanwhile, the Artillery will prevent German reinforcements crossing "No Man's Land", and the Infantry must do their utmost to reconnoitre and locate the exact position held by the enemy, so that our Artillery may bombard the captured trenches with precision: thus further counter attack by our reserves will be executed under the most favourable conditions.

Artillery/

Artillery fire will be opened on the captured trenches without the sanction of the Guards Brigadier concerned.

(f) As regards (e) (iii) :-

It is unlikely that such an attack will come as a surprise, and Commanders will have time to make suitable dispositions.

In any case, no good will be gained by reinforcing the front line.

Supporting troops must hold their ground, and by means of fire and local attacks keep the enemy in check until sufficient reserves are available to assume the offensive.

(g) All Officers must consider the action to be taken by the troops under their command in the event of attack on any portion of the front for the defence of which they are responsible. Plans must be thought out beforehand, and the action to be taken known to all. Nothing should be left to chance.

Battalions and Companies must keep each other informed of their plans to meet various eventualities.

Officers Commanding Battalions in the line will always issue a Defence Scheme to their Company Commanders. This Defence Scheme should be handed over from Battn., to Battn., on relief. It should not contain any information concerning dispositions other than those of the Battn., concerned. A copy will always be sent to Brigade H.Q.,

The action to be taken by Support and Reserve Coy's. in the event of an attack should always be clearly stated, also any special tasks or special points to be defended by Lewis Guns. The action of Reserve Lewis Guns will also be laid down.

It should also be made clear that O.C., Reserve Coy's. must know the position of Units on their right and left, even though they belong to another Division or Brigade.

APPENDIX "B".

GAS ALERT.

When the wind is between N.W. and S.E. Guards Brigades in the line will send the message "ALERT" to all Units under their Command, also to supporting Artillery Group and other attached Units.

The extra precautions to be taken on receipt of this message are as follows :-

EXTRA PRECAUTIONS TO BE TAKEN DURING A GAS ATTACK.

1. All men in positions where they are liable to be suddenly overwhelmed by gas will wear their helmets rolled up and pinned on front of the coat (as per instructions G.D. 1566/G.)

2. A sentry will be posted on every tunnel dugout, or other dugout holding more than 10 men.

3. A sentry will be posted on each group of two or three small dugouts.

4. A sentry will be posted on each Hd.Qrs. and Signal Office.

5. Men sleeping in rearward lines or in works where they are allowed to take off their equipment, will sleep with their gas helmets round their necks, and must know exactly where their second helmet is to be found.

6. All gas helmets will be inspected at the commencement of every "ALERT" period in addition to the ordinary inspection.

7. R.A. sentries will be doubled.

8. An officer on duty will be detailed from each Company in Reserve.

9. Gas helmets must always be worn outside the greatcoat.

10. Men will be forbidden to wear macintosh sheets round their shoulders, and will have the top button of their greatcoats undone.

Daily Intelligence Report
1st Guards Brigade.

8 A.M. Decr. 23rd to 8 A.M. Decr. 24th.

OPERATIONS.

Relief. 2nd Irish Guards relieved 2nd Grenadier Guards as right Battalion. Relief complete by 6-45 P.M.

Patrols. From right Battn. to inspect wire at U 8 d 3.4. Wire here is fairly good.

HOSTILE ACTIVITY.

Front Line. Not much sniping. Enemy Machine Guns fired a few burst during the night. Enemy seemed to be working hard on his front line, digging and baling water.

Artillery. Normal. Shells mostly in rear of our front line at U 8 a 7.5.

Aircraft. Nil.

INTELLIGENCE.

Movement. Party of about 150 observed erecting barbed wire and carrying wood to a trench at O 29 C. They were shelled by our Artillery at 3-15 P.M. and great confusion was caused.

There is an R.E. Dump at the house at O 28 c 6.0. (between ROCQUIGNY and LE MESNIL). Parties leaving here were shelled by our Artillery about 1-20 P.M. and also at 4 P.M. with excellent results.

Large parties seen carrying timber and duck-boards from BARASTRE to O 20 b. Large parties were seen working here all day. An Officer from BARASTRE inspected the work at 10-45. All work stopped and the men stood rigidly to attention.

A tramway is in course of construction about O 19 b (between LE TRANSLOY and VILLERS).

Horsemen were seen laying telephone wires between LE TRANSLOY and BARASTRE.

Trains were seen going between BUS and BARASTRE. The line seems to run North of these Villages.

Wheeled transport seen on the BUS - BARASTRE Road.

Signals. Enemy seem to signal by lamp from O 34 c 8.9. and from U 4 d 10.5 (North and South of LE MESNIL.)

24th Decr. 1916.

Lieut.,
Intelligence Officer, 1st Guards Bde.,

Daily Intelligence Report, 1st Guards Brigade.
----

8 a.m. Decr. 24th 1916 to 8 a.m. Decr. 25th 1916.

OPERATIONS.
- Reliefs. 2nd Bn Coldstream Guards relieved 3rd Bn Coldstream Guards as Left battalion. Relief complete by 7 p.m.
- Patrols. Two patrols went out from Right battalion and reconnoitred "No Man's Land". No enemy patrols were encountered.
- Sniping. Right battalion snipers shot a German, apparently an Officer, who was sketching our trenches from U 8 d 5.3.
- Artillery. At 3.20 p.m. our artillery shelled enemy front line at U 8 d and U 14 b with good effect. At 9 p.m. our retaliation for hostile barrage mostly fell between our front and support lines causing casualties.
- Aircraft. 3 of our aeroplanes over enemy lines at 10.50 a.m. 12 came over again at 3.30 p.m. and although heavily shelled by hostile anti-aircraft guns were not injured.

HOSTILE ACTIVITY.
- Front line. Very little sniping. Machine Guns fired very accurately at reserve trench Left battalion at U 13 a 8.8 at 6 p.m. Enemy seems to be working hard at cleaning out his line.
- Artillery. Considerably above normal. A few 5.9" shells fell near SAILLY CHURCH during morning of 24th. Neighbourhood of the QUARRY shelled about 1.30 p.m. by 4.2's and shrapnel. Observers in enemy front line watch the effect of their shells in SAILLY. About 8.45 p.m. enemy put a barrage of 5.9"'s and shrapnel just in rear of support lines of both Battalions.
- Aircraft. A few enemy aeroplanes over at intervals during the day. They were engaged by anti-aircraft guns., but none were hit. Hostile balloon was up from 1.20 p.m. to 3.45 p.m. behind St Martin's Wood.

INTELLIGENCE.
- Movement. During the day a few Germans came up to and left the front trench in U 14 b. - One man with a bandaged foot was carried to the rear by another man. Small parties of men continually seen about ROCQUIGNY and on the ROCQUIGNY - LUBDA COPSE Road. Wagons were seen taking material from BUS to house at O 28 d 9.2 and then returning between BUS. Trains seen going BARASTRE and BUS and going S.E. for BUS.
- Signals. The hostile barrage in SAILLY at 8.45 p.m. followed red and green lights sent up opposite Left Brigade. However at other times during the night red, green and yellow lights went up with no apparent result. A hostile aeroplane dropped a green light while over our line at 10.30 a.m.
- Locations. Enemy front trench at U 14 b is probably not visible from our front trench but can be seen from support line.

Lieut.
Intelligence Officer, 1st Guards Bde.

Daily Intelligence Report - 1st Guards Bde.,

8 A.M. Decr. 25th to 8 A.M. Decr. 26th.

OPERATIONS.

Reliefs. 1st Irish Guards relieved 2nd Irish Guards as Right Battalion. Relief complete by 6-40 P.M.

Artillery. At 8-30 A.M. and 11-30 A.M. our Artillery bombarded enemy front line. The shooting was good and enemy line seems to be severely damaged.

HOSTILE ACTIVITY.

Front Line. Enemy very quiet except for occasional bursts of M.G. Fire.
He seems to be working hard on his trenches, baling, digging and hammering in stakes.

Artillery. In retaliation for our bombardment, enemy put a few shells near the CHATEAU and also near SAILLY Church. He attempted to retaliate on our front line but his front line troops sent up Green Spray Rockets and the Artillery desisted.
The QUARRY was shelled by 5.9" and shrapnel about 6 P.M.

Aircraft. One enemy aeroplane very high over SAILLY at 7-30 A.M. 26th.

INTELLIGENCE.

Movements. A relief probably took place last night as about 3.0 A.M. parties of enemy were observed moving about on top in U 8 d and wearing packs.
A Company of men seen at 3-20 P.M. marching up to ROCQUIGNY from BUS.
At 10-0 A.M. a party of about 12 men carried planks from ROCQUIGNY to a trench N.W. of LOON Copse. Horse traffic was seen going along BUS - ROCQUIGNY Road.
Trains seen between BUS and ROCQUIGNY and also S.E. of BUS.
The line has been continued from ROCQUIGNY on to LE TRANSLOY and two trains were seen on it.

Locations. A Machine Gun fires at night from the Mound U 2 c 9.1. Two Field Guns seen firing from O 13 b 6.6. (VILLERS.)

MISCELLANEOUS.

A tramway track comes up to a point just E of South end of LOON Copse from round the North side of LE MESNIL.

Miscellaneous. Enemy seen waving a flag from his front trenches at O 36 d.

26th Decr. 1916.

J.H.C. Lieut.,
Intelligence Officer, 1st Guards Bde.,

Daily Intelligence Report.
1st Guards Bde.

8 A.M. Decr. 26th to 8 A.M. Decr. 27th.

OPERATIONS.

Reliefs. 1st Coldstream Guards relieved 2nd Coldstream Guards as left battalion. Relief complete by 6-35 P.M.

Patrols. A patrol of left Battn. went out from U 8 b 2.0 but saw no signs of enemy.

Artillery. Bombarded enemy front line from noon till 4 PM. with excellent results. Considerable activity on part of enemy stretcher bearers observed.

Aircraft. Aircraft very active all the morning (26th). Enemy planes were seen to fall as follows - 9-40 A.M. ST. MALVUS WOOD. 9-45 A.M. Near LE TRANSLOY (by anti-aircraft fire) Nationality unknown. 9-52 RANCOURT. 10-20 Near LE TRANSLOY. One of our Machines came down at 10-5 A.M. about T 18 a.

[MARTINS]

HOSTILE ACTIVITY.

Front line. Enemy very quiet and is busy at baling and cleaning his trench.

Artillery. Activity below normal. A few shells near the CHATEAU in the morning of 26th.

Aircraft. Very active. See OPERATIONS - Aircraft.

INTELLIGENCE.

Movement. Horse traffic was heard during the night from direction of LE MESNIL.

Signals. Enemy seen signalling by lamp from O 29 d (S.W. of BUS.)

During the night Orange and Green Lights went up but nothing happened.

27th Decr. 1916.

Lieut.,
Intelligence Officer, 1st Guards Bde.,

SECRET.

285/a

Copy No. 5

WARNING ORDER.

GUARDS DIVISION ORDER NO. 101.

1. Relief of this Division (less Artillery) by the 20th Division will commence on 1st January, relief to be complete by 10 a.m. 4th January, when the Divn. becomes Corps Reserve.

2. On completion of relief 1st Guards Brigade will be concentrated in MEAULTE - SANDPITS area: Headquarters MEAULTE. 2nd Guards Brigade will be concentrated in CORBIE area: Headquarters CORBIE. 3rd Guards Brigade will be concentrated in VILLE - MERICOURT (2 Battalions) - MEAULTE: Headquarters VILLE. Divisional Headquarters in CORBIE.

3. C.R.E. will arrange relief of Field Coys. R.E. and Pioneers direct. Position of Field Coys. R.E. 20th Division on night of December 31st will be as follows:-

    83rd Field Coy. R.E. less 2 sections   BRONFAY.
    2 sections 83rd Field Coy. R.E.   CARNOY.
    84th Field Coy. R.E.   MEAULTE.
    96th Field Coy. R.E. less 1 section   CORBIE.
    1 section 96th Field Coy. R.E.   DAOURS.

4. A.D.M.S. Guards Division will arrange relief of Field Ambulances direct. Position of Field Ambulances 20th Division on night of December 31st will be as follows:-

    60th Field Ambulance - - CORBIE.
    61st Field Ambulance - - TREUX.
    62nd Field Ambulance - - MEAULTE.

5. Application is being made for the transport of certain Battalions by rail to back area, in addition to the usual train transport from TRONES WOOD Siding to MARICOURT PLATEAU.

ACKNOWLEDGE.

26th December 1916.

Issued to Signals at 11/30 a.m.

Seymour Cpt

for Lieut-Colonel,
General Staff. Guards Divn.

Copy No. 1 General Staff.
       2 "Q".   10 A.D.M.S.
       3 G.D.A.   11 A.D.V.S.
       4 C.R.E.   13 Divnl. Train.
       5 1st Guards Brigade. 14 Senior Supply Officer.
       6 2nd Guards Brigade. 15 O.C. Supply Column.
       7 3rd Guards Brigade. 16 D.A.D.O.S.
       8 Pioneer Battalion. 17 War Diary.
       9 Divnl. Signals.

****

Daily Intelligence Report - 1st Guards Brigade.

8 A.M. Decr. 27th to 8 A.M. Decr. 28th.

OPERATIONS.

Reliefs. 2nd Grenadier Guards relieved 1st Irish Guards as Right Battalion. Relief complete by 7 P.M.

Patrol. A patrol from right Battn. went out from U 8 d 0.2 but saw no signs of enemy.

2 patrols went out from left Battn. U 8 b 1.5 and U 8 b 2.2. They report enemy working hard in their front trench, baling, revetting, etc., and a pump was in work.

HOSTILE ACTIVITY.

Front line. Hostile snipers more active in U 8 b. Enemy hard at work on his front line.

Artillery. Activity below normal. A few shells behind the CHATEAU during the morning and a few shells on BAPAUME Road about U 8 c 6.9. during afternoon of 27th. Mostly 4.2's coming from direction of LE MESNIL.

Gas shells (asphyxiant type) near COMBLES Cemetery during the night.

Aircraft. Active during morning of 27th. One hostile plane low over the QUARRY about noon. Two planes over SAILLY about 7-45 A.M. 28th. A parachute drifted over from East of SAILLISEL and landed 11-20 A.M. 27th about T 11 b. There was no occupant.

INTELLIGENCE.

Relief. A enemy relief may have taken place last night as much splashing in the mud was heard.

Movement. Men being carried on stretchers were observed in U 9 and along road at U 3 c. Probably the result of our Artillery fire.

A digging party was seen working at U 3 c.

BUS. A train was observed going between BARASTRE and BUS. The day was too misty for good observation.

Signal. During the last two nights the enemy has sent up much fewer Very Lights.

28th Decr. 1916.

Intelligence Officer, 1st Guards Bde.,

Lieut.,

Daily Intelligence Report - 1st Guards Bde.

8 A.M. Dec: 29th to 8 A.M. Dec: 30th.

OPERATIONS.

Relief. 2nd Bn. Irish Guards relieved 2nd Bn. Grenadier Guards in the right sector. Relief complete by 7-15 P.M.

Sniping. Left Battalion claim 5 Germans, two of these were apparently Artillery observers, two were in the enemy trenches and one was an enemy sniper lying in front of his parapet.

Patrols. No patrols went out.

HOSTILE ACTIVITY.

Front Line. Very little sniping. One man was seen to fire through a plate about U 8 b 3.0.
From 10 A.M. onwards enemy was observed throwing bombs in front of his trench about U 8 d 6.3. perhaps testing them.
At midday some Rifle Grenades were fired over our trenches about U 14 b 5.5.

Artillery. Enemy Artillery was very active during the day, the Northern part of SAILLY being the principal target.
In retaliation for our bombardment the front line of right Battalion was immediately shelled and a sprinkling of H.E. and Shrapnel was fired into SAILLY.
At 6-45 P.M. the Village especially about U 14 a was heavily barraged.

Aircraft. Nil.

INTELLIGENCE.

Movement. At 12 noon men were seen pushing two trucks, apparently laden with rails, along a tramway which runs from N.E. corner of ROCQUIGNY towards LUBDA COPSE.
At 11-40 A.M. a train was seen travelling from VILLERS-AU-FLOS, passing behind BARASTRE and was lost to view behind BUS. At 2-25 P.M. a second train followed along the same route.
At 2-30 P.M. two six horse wagons came out of ROCQUIGNY travelling towards VILLERS.
Enemy was hard at work all day on his front and support lines; some appeared to be wearing a F.S. Cap with white band, others a cap with reddish band. It was noted that hardly any men behind the lines carried rifles. A dachshund was seen circling round a shell hole most of the day, this hole was kept under fire and it is believed that one or two Germans were hiding there.

Location. Many Germans were seen and much work was being done near a large mound of new earth between LONELY HOUSE at O 28 c 6.0. and ROCQUIGNY, this position requires further verification.

Signals. While SAILLY was being barraged at 6-45 P.M. some German shells fell short, a Green Very Light was immediately sent up and the range was lengthened. Red, Green and Yellow Lights were sent up at intervals during the night by the enemy, but no results were observed. Green flares were sent up by the enemy during our bombardment.

N.B. Rain fell continuously throughout the night and the trench

286/a

Copy No... 5..

GUARDS DIVISION ORDER NO. 102.

(a) The Division (less Artillery) will be relieved by the 20th Division (less Artillery) commencing on the night 1st/2nd January and finishing by 10 a.m. on the 4th January.

(b) On relief, the Division will be concentrated in the area SANDPITS - MEAULTE - VILLE - MERICOURT - CORBIE, and will become Division in Corps Reserve.

2. (a) One front line battalion Right Group and one front line battalion Left Group will be relieved by one battalion 61st Inf. Bde. and by one battalion 60th Inf. Bde. respectively on night 2nd/3rd January.

(b) One front line battalion Right Group and one front line battalion Left Group will be relieved by one battalion 61st Inf. Bde. and by one battalion 60th Inf. Bde. respectively on night 3rd/4th January.

(c) 3rd Guards Brigade M.G.Company & T.M.Battery from left sector will be relieved on night 1st/2nd January by 59th Inf. Bde. M.G.Company & T.M.Battery.

2nd Guards Brigade M.G.Company & T.M.Battery from right sector will be relieved on night 2nd/3rd January by 61st Inf. Bde. M.G.Company & T.M.Battery.

3. Details of reliefs will be settled direct between Brigades concerned.

4. Moves of Guards Brigades into XIV Corps Reserve Area are shewn in Appendix 'A' attached.

5. Distribution on completion of relief is shewn in Appendix 'B'.

6. Table of routes and hours of starting will be issued later.

7. (a) C.R.E. will arrange details of relief of Field Coys.R.E. and Pioneer Battalion, the latter taking over the work of

/Pioneer

Pioneer Battalion 20th Division, under C.E., XIV Corps on January 3rd 1917 and will be located in MONTAUBAN.

(b) A.D.M.S. will arrange details of relief of Medical Units with A.D.M.S., 20th Division.

In both cases the arrangements made will be notified to this office.

8. Defence Scheme - Secret Maps and Air Photographs will be handed over to relieving Brigades.

9. All trench stores will be handed over on relief, receipts taken, and lists in accordance with G.D. No. 1141/A dated 27th December, sent to Divisional Headquarters.

10. All orders for the movements of battalions in the Right and Left Groups will be issued by G.OsC., Right and Left Groups respectively. G.O.C., 3rd Guards Brigade will assume command of units comprising 3rd Guards Brigade on their arrival in 3rd Guards Brigade area.

11. The Division will take over all working parties now found by the 20th Division in accordance with instructions that are being issued separately.

12. Orders as regards entrainment for troops that are moving by rail will be issued by "Q".

13. G.Os.C., 1st and 2nd Guards Brigades will hand over command of their Sectors to G.Os.C., 61st and 59th Inf. Bdes. respectively on completion of the relief in those sectors.

G.O.C., 3rd Guards Brigade will hand over command of Divisional Reserve at 12 noon on 3rd January to G.O.C., 60th Inf. Bde.

14. G.O.C., Guards Division will hand over command of the line to G.O.C., 20th Division at 10 a.m. on 4th January 1917 at which hour Divisional Headquarters will close at ARROWHEAD COPSE and open at CORBIE.

/15.

15.   The Division (less Artillery) will be prepared to move to Area 3, changing places with the 29th Division (less Artillery).

This move will commence on January 10th under orders to be issued later.

ACKNOWLEDGE.

E Seymour
Captain,
for Lieut-Colonel,
General Staff, Guards Division.

26th December 1916.

Issued to Signals at 8 p.m.

Copy No. 1 General Staff.   12 A.P.M.
         2 "Q".   13 Divnl. Train.
         3 C.D.A.   14 Senior Supply Officer.
         4 C.R.E.   15 O.C., Supply Column.
         5 1st Guards Brigade. 16 D.A.D.O.S.
         6 2nd Guards Brigade. 17 O.C. Sanitary Section.
         7 3rd Guards Brigade. 18 4th Division.
         8 Pioneer Battalion. 19 17th Division.
         9 Divnl. Signals.   20 20th Division.
        10 A.D.M.S.   21 XIV Corps.
        11 A.D.V.S.   22 War Diary.

****

Appendix 'A'.

MOVEMENTS OF BATTALIONS OF GUARDS DIVISION DURING RELIEF.

Date.	Unit.	From.	Destination.	Remarks.
Jany.1.	1/Coldstream Guards.	COMBLES area.	LINE.	
	1/Scots Guards.	BOULEAUX area.	LINE.	
	2/Coldstream Guards.	LINE.	BRONFAY	Rail.
	2/Scots Guards.	LINE.	BRONFAY	Rail.
	3/Coldstream Guards.	BRONFAY.	MEAULTE.	
	2/Grenadier Guards.	BRONFAY.	MEAULTE.	
	1/Welsh Guards.	BRONFAY.	YILLE,	
	1st Gds.Bde.M.G.Coy.	BRONFAY.	MEAULTE,	
	1st Gds.Bde.T.M.Baty.	BRONFAY.	MEAULTE.	
	3rd Gds.Bde.M.G.Coy.	LINE.	BRONFAY	Rail.
	3rd Gds.Bde.T.M.Baty.	LINE.	BRONFAY	Rail.
Jany.2.	2/Irish Guards.	MALTZHORN.	CORBIE	Rail.
	4/Grenadier Guards.	MALTZHORN.	MEAULTE.	
	1/Grenadier Guards.	BRONFAY.	MERICOURT.	
	1/Irish Guards.	LINE.	BRONFAY,	

Continued.

Page 2.

Date.	Unit.	From.	Destination.	Remarks.
Jany.2.	3/Grenadier Guards.	LINE.	CORBIE	Rail.
	2nd Gds.Bde.M.G.Coy.	LINE.	CORBIE	Rail.
	2nd Gds.Bde.T.M.Baty.	LINE.	CORBIE	Rail.
	76th Field Coy.R.E.	COMBLES.	CORBIE	Rail.
Jany.3.	1/Irish Guards.	BRONFAY.	SANDPITS.	
	2/Coldstream Guards.	BRONFAY.	MEAULT E.	
	2/Scots Guards.	BRONFAY.	MERICOURT.	
	1/Coldstream Guards.	LINE.	CORBIE	Rail.
	1/Scots Guards.	LINE.	CORBIE	Rail.
	3rd Gds.Bde.M.G.Coy.	BRONFAY.	VILLE.	
	3rd Gds.Bde.T.M.Baty.	BRONFAY. LINE	VILLE. MEAULTE	

Appendix 'B'.

DISTRIBUTION OF GUARDS BRIGADES
on completion of relief.

SANDPITS.	MEAULTE.	MERICOURT.	VILLE.	CORBIE.
1/Irish Guards.	Hd.Qrs. 1st Guards Brigade. 2/Grenadier Guards. 2/Coldstream Guards. 3/Coldstream Guards. 4/Grenadier Guards. 1st Gds.Bde.M.G.Coy & T.M.Battery.	2/Scots Guards. 1/Grenadier Gds.	Hd.Qrs. 3rd Guards Brigade. 1/Welsh Guards. 3rd Gds.Bde.M.G.Coy & T.M.Battery.	Hd.Qrs. 2nd Guards Brigade. 1/Coldstream Guards. 2/Irish Guards. 1/Scots Guards. 3/Grenadier Guards. 2nd Gds.Bde.M.G.Coy & T.M.Battery.

G.D. No. 2674/G.

S E C R E T.

"Q".	4th Division.
G.D.A.	17th Division.
C.R.E.	20th Division.
1st Guards Brigade.	XIV Corps.
2nd Guards Brigade.	Camp Jomdts.
3rd Guards Brigade.	MALTZHORN.
Pioneer Battalion.	CAMP "15" BRONFAY.
Divnl. Signals.	CAMP "108" BRONFAY.
A.D.M.S.	SANDPITS.
A.D.V.S.	Town Majors.
A.P.M.	MERICOURT.
Divnl. Train.	VILLE.
Senior Supply Officer.	CORBIE.
O.C. Supply Column.	COMBLES.
D.A.D.O.S.	Meaulte
O.C. Sanitary Section.	

Reference Guards Division Order No. 102, para: 6, Table of routes and hours of starting, marked Appendix "C", is attached.

All troops on roads East of MEAULTE (inclusive) will move in file with intervals of 200 yards between Companies and 500 yards between Battalions.

All units whose transport is ordered to use the BERNAFAY - MARICOURT road in a Southerly direction, will obtain passes to do so from A.P.M. Guards Division, in accordance with D.R.O. 1888, dated 11/12/16.

A C K N O W L E D G E.

E Seymour.
Captain,
General Staff. Guards Divn.

28th December 1916.

APPENDIX "C".
****

1.

DATE.	UNIT.	FROM.	TO.	ROUTE.	TRANSPORT.	REMARKS.
1st Jan.	3rd Cold.Gds.	BRONFAY.	MEAULTE.	BRAY - FORKED TREE	MARICOURT - FRICOURT CEMETERY. Leaves transport lines at 11 a.m.	Bn. to clear CAMP "103" at 10 a.m.
	2nd Gren.Gds.	BRONFAY.	MEAULTE.	BRAY - FORKED TREE	MARICOURT - FRICOURT CEMETERY. Leaves transport lines at 11.30 a.m.	Bn. to clear CAMP "15" at 10.30 a.m.
	1st Welsh Gds.	BRONFAY.	VILLE.	BRAY - MORLANCOURT.	Follows in rear of Bn.	Bn. to clear CAMP "15" at 11 a.m.
	1st Guards Bde. M.G.Coy. and T.M.Batt.	BRONFAY.	MEAULTE.	BRAY - FORKED TREE.	MARICOURT - FRICOURT CEMETERY. Leaves transport lines at 11.30 a.m.	To clear CAMP at 11.30 a.m.

2.

DATE.	UNIT.	FROM.	TO.	ROUTE.	TRANSPORT.	REMARKS
	1st Gren. Gds.	MALTZHORN.	MERICOURT.	BRAY - Cross roads at J.22.b.	To follow unit.	Bn. to clear MALTZHORN CAMP * at 10.30 a.m.
	4th Gren. Gds.	BRONFAY.	HEAULTE.	MARICOURT - FRICOURT CEMETERY.	BRAY - SANDPITS. To leave transport lines 11 a.m.	Bn. to clear "CAMP 15" at 10 a.m. ✗
	2nd Irish Gds. (Personnel).	MALTZHORN.	CORBIE Night 2/3.	Rail.	BRAY - CORBIE. To leave transport lines 6 a.m.	Bn. to clear MALTZHORN CAMP by 6 p.m.
	3rd Gren. Gds. (Personnel).	LINE.	—do—	Rail.	Same route. To leave transport lines 6.15 a.m.	
	2nd Gds.Bde. M.G.Coy. & T.M. Batt. (Personnel).	LINE.	—do—	Rail.	Same route. To leave transport lines 6.30 a.m.	
	76th Field Coy. R.E.	CATACOMBS.	CORBIE.	Rail.		C.R.E. will issue instructions for movements of personnel and transport.
2nd Jan.	4th Cold.Gds. (Pioneers).	WEDGE WOOD.	MONTAUBAN.			—do—
	75th Field Coy. R.E.	CATACOMBS.				—do—
	55th Field Coy. R.E.	WEDGE WOOD.				—do—

* Not BRONFAY CAMP as laid down in Guards Divn. Order No.102, Appendix "A"

✗ Not MALTZHORN CAMP as laid down in Guards Divn. Order No.102, Appendix "A".

DATE	UNIT.	FROM.	TO.	ROUTE.	TRANSPORT.	REMARKS.
	1st Irish Gds.	BRONFAY.	SANDPITS.	BRAY.	To follow unit.	Bn. to clear CAMP "108" by 3 p.m.
	2nd Scots Gds.	BRONFAY.	MERICOURT.	BRAY - cross roads at J.22.b.	To follow unit.	Bn. to clear CAMP "15" at 10 a.m.
	2nd Cold. Gds.	BRONFAY.	MEAULTE.	BRAY - FORKED TREE.	MARICOURT - FRICOURT CEMETERY. To leave at 10.30 a.m. transport lines 11 am	Bn. to clear CAMP "15" at 10.30 a.m.
3rd Jan.	1st Cold. Gds. (Personnel).	LINE.	CORBIE, Night 3/4 Jan.	Rail.	(BRAY - CORBIE. To (leave transport (lines 6 a.m.	
	1st Scots Gds. (Personnel).	LINE.	CORBIE, Night 3/4 Jan.	Rail.	(BRAY - CORBIE. To (leave transport (lines 6.15 a.m.	
	3rd Gds.Bde. M.G.Coy. and T.M.Batt.	BRONFAY.	VILLE.	BRAY - MORLANCOURT.	To follow unit.	To clear Camp at 11 a.m.

Daily Intelligence Report — 1st Guards Bde.,

8 A.M. Decr. 28th to 8 A.M. Decr. 29th.

OPERATIONS.

Reliefs. 3rd Coldstream Guards relieved 1st Coldstream Guards as left Battalion. Relief complete by 6-35 P.M.

Sniping. 3 Germans were shot, 1 by left Battn. and 2 by right Battn.

HOSTILE ACTIVITY.

Front Line. A little sniping opposite right Battalion. A Machine Gun fired fairly accurately at our parapet at U 14 b 3.9 and U 8 d 0.1.

Artillery. Eight salvos of 5.9's into SAILLY about midday from behind LE MESNIL.

Aircraft. Very active. Two low over SAILLY about 7-30 A.M. 28th. One of these fired on our front line with a Machine Gun and after dropping a blue light, flew back. Five more planes were seen about 9 A.M. flying towards LE TRANSLOY and there were 14 up about noon all flying high.

INTELLIGENCE.

Movement. Small parties were seen road mending between LE TRANSLOY and ROCQUIGNY and more were seen working a windlass at O 26 b 1.2. The weather was unfavourable for good observation.

Signals. Hostile plane dropped a blue light over SAILLY on morning of 28th.
Enemy sent up two Green Lights from U 1 a 9.9 which were answered by a single Green light 500 yards further North (South of LE TRANSLOY.) No artillery action followed.

Locations. There is a small mound resembling a Machine Gun emplacement at U 9.0 3.2.

Jack

Lieut.,
Intelligence Officer, 1st Guards Brigade.

29th Decr: 1916.

S E C R E T.   Copy No. 23

1st Guards Brigade Order No. 95.

Ref. Map - ALBERT 1/40,000.   29th Decr: 1916.

1. The Right Guards Brigade Group will be relieved by Right Brigade Group of 20th Division in accordance with attached table.

2. Until completion of relief Battn's. of 1st Guards Brigade in MEAULTE Area will come under Orders of G.O.C., 61st Infantry Brigade.
   Similarly Battn's. of 61st Infantry Brigade will come under Orders of G.O.C., Right Guards Brigade Group.

3. Details of relief not laid down herein, will be arranged direct between O.C's concerned.
   Any Units of 2nd Guards Brigade requiring Transport to move from the Line, COMBLES or MALTZHORN to TRONES Wood Station, will apply to this Office 48 hours previously.

4. All Trench Stores, Air Photographs, Secret Maps, Brigade Defence Scheme and Orders relating to the present Sector will be handed over to relieving Units by 1st Coldstream Guards, 1st Irish Guards, 2nd Gds.Bde. M.G.Company and 2nd Gds.Bde. T.M.Battery on relief in the Front Line.
   Other Units will forward any of the above in their possession to Group H.Q., before they move back into the MEAULTE Area.
   Receipts for Trench Stores handed over will be forwarded to 1st Guards Brigade I.O., in duplicate on the forms sent to Units concerned as soon as possible after relief.

5. Billeting Parties of 1st and 2nd Guards Brigades will report to the Town Majors of MEAULTE and CORBIE respectively on the day on which Units move into these Areas. They should report at least 4 hours before their Units are due to arrive.

6. Cookers will be moved to rejoin their Units as follows :-

   Jan: 1st.

       2nd G.G. from BRONFAY 15 with Battn. to MEAULTE.

       2nd C.G. from COMBLES to BRONFAY 15 after teas.

       2nd I.G. from BRONFAY 108 to Transport Lines 2nd I.G.

   Jan: 2nd.

       1st I.G. from MALTZHORN to BRONFAY 108.

       1st C.G. will rejoin their Transport Lines.

7/

7. The 8 pack animals belonging to Battn's. will rejoin their 1st Line Transport on the day previous to that on which Battn's. move into the MEAULTE or CORBIE Area.

The extra horses now in COMBLES will rejoin their 1st Line on Dec: 31st.

8. All tools and S.A.A. will be dumped in the Transport Lines under arrangements to be made by the Bde. Transport Officer. Receipts will be forwarded in duplicate to this Office.

9. Gum boots and water tins will be handed in to the Gum Boot Store by Battn's. coming out of the Line in the usual way.

10. On January 1st the blankets in Camp 15 will be divided equally between the 2nd Grenadier Guards and 2nd Coldstream Guards.

Similarly those in Camp 108 will be divided between the 3rd Coldstream Guards and 1st Irish Guards, and those in MALTZHORN between the 1st Coldstream Guards and 2nd Irish Guards.

From January 1st each Battn. is responsible for the care and removal of its blankets to the new Area.

All blankets in COMBLES Area will be collected by 1st Coldstream Guards on morning of Jan: 1st and handed in to Gum Boot Store in COMBLES.

11. No extra Transport is available for the move. The 1st Coldstream Guards and 2nd Irish Guards will make their own arrangements for moving blankets from MALTZHORN to TRONES Wood Siding in order to catch the train by which the personnel is travelling.

12. Sapping Platoons will rejoin their Battn's. on the day before their Battn's. move into the MEAULTE or CORBIE Area. Transport will be arranged for by Battn's.

13. 1st Guards Brigade H.Q., will close at COMBLES and open at MEAULTE on completion of relief.

ACKNOWLEDGE.

M.B. Smith

Captain,
Brigade Major, 1st Guards Brigade.

Issued through Signals at -

Copy No. 1. 2nd Grenadier Gds.
2. 1st Coldstream Gds.
3. 2nd Coldstream Gds.
4. 3rd Coldstream Gds.
5. 1st Irish Gds.
6. 2nd Irish Gds.
7. 1st Gds.Bde.M.G.Coy.
8. 1st Gds.Bde.T.M.Bty.
9. Guards Division.
10. 2nd Guards Brigade.

Copy No. 11. 10th Infantry Brigade.
12. Right Group Artillery.
13. 75th Field Coy. R.E.
14. Bde. Transport Officer.
15. Bde. Supply Officer.
16. Town Major, MEAULTE.
17. Camp Commdt., BRONFAY.
18. " " MALTZHORN.
19. Staff Captain.
20. C.O., Signals.
20 - 25 Retained.

Date.	Unit.	From.	To.	Remarks.
31st 1916.	1st Cold.Gds.	CORBIE.	Left Sub-sector.	Not to pass HAIE Wood before 5-30PM.
	2nd Cold.Gds.	Left Sub-sector.	BRONFAY Camp 15.	Train leaves TRONES Wood for PLATEAU not later than 2 A.M.
	3rd Cold.Gds.	BRONFAY 108.	MEAULTE.	(a) Battn. to clear Camp 108 by 10 A.M. Route BRAY – FORKED TREE (L.2–a.) (b) Transport to leave transport lines at 11 A.M. Route MARICOURT – FRICOURT Cemetery.
	2nd Gren.Gds.	BRONFAY Camp 15.	MEAULTE.	(a) Battn. to clear Camp 15 at 10-30 A.M. Route BRAY – FORKED TREE (L.2–a.) (b) Transport to leave transport lines at 11-20 A.M. Route MARICOURT – FRICOURT Cemetery.
	1st Gds.Bde. H.G.Coy. & T.M.Bty.	BRONFAY.	MEAULTE.	(a) To clear camp at 11-30 A.M. Route BRAY – FORKED TREE Camp (L.2.a) (b) Transport to leave transport lines at 11-30 A.M. Route MARICOURT and FRICOURT Cemetery. (c) H.G.Coy. to provide transport for T.M.Bty.

Unit.	From.	To.	Remarks.
2nd Irish Gds.	MALTZHORN.	CORBIE.	(a) Train leaves TRONES Wood Siding for CORBIE at 6 P.M. (b) Transport to leave Transport Lines at 5 A.M. Route BRAY - CORBIE.
2nd Gds.Bde. M.G.Coy. & T.M.Bty.	Line.	CORBIE.	(a) Relief will not pass COMBLES Cemetery before 6 P.M. (b) Train leaves TRONES Wood Siding for CORBIE at 2 A.M. night of 2nd/3rd Jan: (c) Transport to leave transport lines at 6-30 A.M. Jan.2nd. Route BRAY - CORBIE. (d) Relieving C.O's will come up on Dec:31st.
1st Irish Gds.	Right Sub-sector.	BRONFAY 108.	(a) Relieved by 7th Somerset L.I. (b) Relieving troops not to pass HAIE Wood before 5-30 P.M. (c) Officers of relieving Unit will visit Battn. H.Q. on Jan: 1st - time to be notified later. (d) Train leaves TRONES Wood Siding for PLATEAU not later than 2 A.M. (e) Further details re guides etc. to be arranged direct.

Date.	Unit.	From.	To.	Remarks.
Jan:3rd.	1st Irish Gds.	Bronfay. 1.8.	SANDPITS.	(a) To clear Camp 108 at 3 P.M. Route via BRAY. (b) Transport to march in rear of Unit.
	2/d Cold.Gds.	BRONFAY. 15.	MEAULTE.	(a) To clear Camp 15 at 10-30 A.M. Route BRAY - FORKED TREE L.2.8. (b) Transport to leave transport lines at 11 A.M. Route MARICOURT - FRICOURT Cemetery.
	1st Cold.Gds.	Left Sub-sector.	CORBIE.	(a) Relieved by 12th Kings. (b) Relieving troops not to pass HAIE Wood before 5-30 P.M. (c) Officers of relieving Unit will visit Battn. H.Q. on Jan:2nd. Time to be notified later. (d) Train leaves TRONES Wood Siding for CORBIE not later than 2 A.M. night of Jan: 3rd/4th. (e) Details 're' guides etc. to be arranged direct. (f) Transport to leave Transport Lines at 6 A.M. Route BRAY - CORBIE.

SECRET.　　　　　　　　　　　　　　　　　　Copy No ..5..

288/A

GUARDS DIVISION ORDER NO. 103.

Guards Division Order No. 102 and Appendices is cancelled

1. (a) The Division (less Artillery) will be relieved by the 20th Division (less Artillery) from U.1.d.6.6 to present right of Division, commencing on the night 1st/2nd January, and finishing by 10 a.m. on the 4th January.

   (b) One Battalion 17th Division will relieve the Division as far as U.1.d.6.6. Relief to be complete by 8 a.m. on January 4th.

   (c) On relief the Division will be concentrated in the area SANDPITS - MEAULTE - VILLE - MERICOURT - CORBIE and will become Division in Corps Reserve.

2. (a) <u>Night 1st/2nd January.</u>

   3rd Guards Brigade M.G.Coy. and T.M.Batt. from Left Sector will be relieved by 59th M.G.Coy. in the right sub-sector and by the 52nd M.G.Coy. in the left sub-sector.

   (b) <u>Night 2nd/3rd January.</u>

   1st Bn. Irish Guards
   (from front line Right Group) will be relieved by) One Battalion 61st Inf.Bde.

   3rd Bn. Grenadier Gds.
   (from front line Left Group) will be relieved by) One Battalion 60th Inf.Bde.

   1st Bn. Scots Guards
   (from front line Left Group) will be relieved by) One Battalion 52nd Inf.Bde.
                                                     (17th Division).
   This Battalion comes under the command of G.O.C. 52nd Inf. Bde. when relief is complete.

   2nd Guards Bde.
   M.G.Coy. and T.M.Batt.
   (from Right Group) will be relieved by) 61st M.G.Coy. and T.M.Batt.

   (c) <u>Night 3rd/4th January.</u>

   1st Bn. Coldstream Gds.
   (from front line Right Group) will be relieved by) One Battalion 61st Inf.Bde.

   (d) The 20th Division will relieve the left of the 8th Division as far as U.20.b.6.6 on the night 3rd/4th Jany.

2.

3. Details of reliefs will be settled direct between Brigades concerned.

4. Moves of Guards Brigades into XIV Corps Reserve Area are shewn in Appendix "A" attached.

5. Distribution on completion of relief is shewn in Appendix "B" attached.

6. Table of routes and hours of starting is shewn in Appendix "C" attached.

7. (a) C.R.E. will arrange details of relief of Field Coys. R.E. and Pioneer Battalion, the latter taking over the work of Pioneer Battalion, 20th Division, under C.E., XIV Corps on January 3rd 1917.

(b) A.D.M.S. will arrange details of relief of medical units with A.D.M.S. 20th Division.

8. Defence Schemes Secret maps and air photographs will be handed over to relieving Brigades 20th Division, and Secret maps and air photographs to relieving Battalion 17th Division in so far as they affect the left sub-sector of the Left Group.

9. All trench stores will be handed over on relief; receipts taken, and lists (in accordance with G.D. No.1141/A dated 27th December) sent to Divisional Headquarters.

10. All orders for movements to back area will be issued by G.Os.C. Right and Left Groups respectively. G.O.C. 3rd Guards Brigade will resume command of 3rd Guards Brigade on their arrival in VILLE - MERICOURT - MEAULTE area.

11. All working parties now found by 20th Division will be taken over under instructions already issued.

12. Orders as regards entrainment of troops have been issued by "Q".

13. G.O.C. Left Group will hand over command on completion of relief on night 2nd/3rd to G.O.C. 59th Inf. Bde.

3.

G.O.C. Right Group will hand over command on completion of relief on night 3rd/4th to G.O.C. 61st Inf. Bde.

G.O.C. 3rd Guards Brigade will hand over command of Divisional Reserve at 12 noon on 3rd January to G.O.C. 60th Inf. Bde.

14. G.O.C. Guards Division will hand over command of the line to G.O.C. 20th Division at 10 a.m. on 4th January, at which hour Divisional Headquarters will close at ARROWHEAD COPSE and re-open at CORBIE.

15. The Division (less Artillery) will be prepared to move to Area 3 changing places with the 29th Division (less Artillery).

This move will commence on January 10th, under orders to be issued later.

ACKNOWLEDGE.

E Seymour
Captain,
General Staff, Guards Divn.

31st December 1916.

Issued to Signals at 8 p.m.

Copy No.				
1	General Staff.	18	8th Division.
2	"Q".	19	17th Division.
3	G.D.A.	20	20th Division.
4	C.R.E.	21	XIV Corps.
5	1st Guards Brigade.	22	Camp Comdt. MALTZHORN.
6	2nd Guards Brigade.	23	-do- CAMP "15".
7	3rd Guards Brigade.	24	-do- CAMP "108".
8	Pioneer Battalion.	25	-do- SANDPITS.
9	Divnl. Signals.	26	-do- MANSEL CAMP.
10	A.D.M.S.	27	Town Major, MERICOURT.
11	A.D.V.S.	28	-do- VILLE.
12	A.P.M.	29	-do- CORBIE.
13	Divnl. Train.	30	-do- OCMELES.
14	Senior Supply Officer.	31	-do- MEAULTE.
15	O.C. Supply Column.	32	War Diary.
16	D.A.D.O.S.		
17	O.C. Sanitary Section.		

****

APPENDIX "A".
****

MOVEMENTS OF BATTALIONS OF GUARDS DIVISION DURING RELIEF.
****

DATE.	UNIT.	FROM.	DESTINATION.	REMARKS.
Jan.1st.	1/Coldstream Guards.	COMBLES Area.	LINE.	
	1/Scots Guards.	BOULEAUX Area.	LINE.	
	2/Coldstream Guards.	LINE.	BRONFAY............	Rail.
	2/Scots Guards.	LINE.	BRONFAY............	Rail.
	3/Coldstream Guards.	BRONFAY.	MEAULTE.	
	2/Grenadier Guards.	BRONFAY.	MEAULTE.	
	1/Welsh Guards.	BRONFAY.	VILLE.	
	1st Gds.Bde.M.G.Coy.	BRONFAY.	MEAULTE.	
	1st Gds.Bde.T.M.Batt.	BRONFAY.	MEAULTE.	
	3rd Gds.Bde.M.G.Coy.	LINE.	BRONFAY............	Rail.
	3rd Gds.Bde.T.M.Batt.	LINE.	BRONFAY............	Rail.
Jan.2nd.	2/Irish Guards.	MALTZHORN.	CORBIE.............	Rail.
	4/Grenadier Guards.	BRONFAY.	MERICOURT.	
	1/Grenadier Guards.	MALTZHORN.	MEAULTE.	
	1/Irish Guards.	LINE.	BRONFAY............	Rail.

Continued.

Page 2.

DATE.	UNIT.	FROM.	DESTINATION.	REMARKS.
Jan.2nd.	3/Grenadier Guards.	LINE.	CORBIE.	Rail.
	2nd Gds.Bde.M.G.Coy.	LINE.	CORBIE.	Rail.
	2nd Gds.Bde.T.M.Batt.	LINE.	CORBIE.	Rail.
	76th Field Coy. R.E.	COMBLES.	CORBIE.	Rail.
	1/Scots Guards.	LINE.	CORBIE.	Rail.
Jan.3rd.	1/Irish Guards.	BRONFAY.	SANDPITS.	
	2/Coldstream Guards.	BRONFAY.	MEAULTE.	
	2/Scots Guards.	BRONFAY.	MERICOURT.	
	1/Coldstream Guards.	LINE.	CORBIE.	Rail.
	3rd Gds.Bde.M.G.Coy.	BRONFAY.	VILLE.	
	3rd Gds.Bde.T.M.Batt.	BRONFAY.	VILLE.	

APPENDIX "B".

DISTRIBUTION OF GUARDS BRIGADES
ON COMPLETION OF RELIEF.

SANDPITS.	MEAULTE.	MERICOURT.	VILLE.	CORBIE.
1/Irish Guards.	Hd.Qrs. 1st Guards Bde. 2/Grenadier Guards. 2/Coldstream Guards. 3/Coldstream Guards. 1/Grenadier Guards. 1st Gds.Bde. M.G.Coy. and T.M.Batt.	2/Scots Guards. 4/Grenadier Guards.	H.Q. 3rd Guards Bde. 1/Welsh Guards. 3rd Gds.Bde. M.G.Coy. and T.M.Batt.	H.Q. 2nd Guards Bde. 1/Coldstream Guards. 2/Irish Guards. 1/Scots Guards. 3/Grenadier Guards. 2nd Gds.Bde. M.G.Coy. and T.M.Batt.

APPENDIX "C".

DATE.	UNIT.	FROM.	TO.	ROUTE.	TRANSPORT.	REMARKS.
1st Jan.	3rd Cold.Gds.	BRONFAY.	MEAULTE.	BRAY - FORKED TREE	MARICOURT - FRICOURT CEMETERY. Leaves transport lines at 11 a.m.	Bn. to clear CAMP "108" at 10 a.m.
	2nd Gren.Gds.	BRONFAY.	MEAULTE.	BRAY - FORKED TREE.	MARICOURT - FRICOURT CEMETERY. Leaves transport lines at 11.20 a.m.	Bn. to clear CAMP "15" at 10.45 a.m.
	1st Welch Gds.	BRONFAY.	VILLE.	BRAY - MORLANCOURT.	Follows in rear of Bn.	Bn. to clear CAMP "15" at 11 a.m.
	1st Guards Bde. M.G.Coy. and T.M.Batt.	BRONFAY.	MEAULTE.	BRAY - FORKED TREE.	MARICOURT - FRICOURT CEMETERY. Leaves transport lines at 11.30 a.m.	To clear CAMP at 11.30 a.m.

2.

DATE.	UNIT.	FROM.	TO.	ROUTE.	TRANSPORT.	REMARKS.
	1st Gren. Gds.	MALTZHORN.	MEAULTE.	MARICOURT - FRICOURT CEMETERY.	To follow unit.	Bn. to clear MALTZHORN CAMP at 10.30 a.m.
	4th Gren. Gds.	BRONFAY.	MERICOURT.	BRAY - Cross roads at J.22.b.	BRAY - Cross roads at J.22.b. To leave transport lines 11 a.m.	Bn. to clear CAMP "15" at 10 a.m.
	2nd Irish Gds. (Personnel).	MALTZHORN	CORBIE Night 2/3.	Rail.	BRAY - CORBIE. To leave transport lines 6 a.m.	Bn. to clear MALTZHORN CAMP by 5 p.m.
	3rd Gren. Gds. (Personnel).	LINE.	--do--	Rail.	Same route. To leave transport lines 6.15 a.m.	
	1st Scots Gds. (Personnel).	LINE.	--do--	Rail.	Same route. To leave transport lines 6.30 a.m.	
2nd Jan.	2nd Gds.Bde. M.G.Coy.& T.M. Batt.(Personnel)	LINE.	--do--	Rail.	Same route. To leave transport lines 5.45 a.m.	
	75th Field Coy. R.E.	CATACOMBS.	CORBIE.	Rail.		C.R.E. will issue instructions for movements of personnel and transport.
	75th Field Coy. R.E.	CATACOMBS.				--do--
	55th Field Coy. R.E.	WEDGE WOOD.				--do--

DATE.	UNIT.	FROM.	TO.	ROUTE.	TRANSPORT.	REMARKS.
	1st Irish Gds.	BRONFAY.	SANDPITS.	BRAY.	To follow unit.	Bn. to clear CAMP "108" by 3 p.m.
	2nd Scots Gds.	BRONFAY.	MERICOURT.	BRAY - Cross roads at J.22.b.	To follow unit.	Bn. to clear CAMP "15" at 10 a.m.
	2nd Cold.Gds.	BRONFAY.	MEAULTE.	BRAY - FORKED TREE.	MARICOURT - FRICOURT CEMETERY. To leave transport lines 11 a.m.	Bn. to clear CAMP "15" at 10.30 a.m.
3rd Jan.	1st Cold.Gds. (Personnel).	LIKE.	CORBIE. Night 3/4 Jan.	Rail.	BRAY - CORBIE. To leave transport lines 8 a.m.	
	4th Cold.Gds. (Pioneers).	WEDGE WOOD.	MONTAUBAN.			C.R.E. will issue instructions for movements of personnel and transport.
	3rd Gds.Bde. M.G.Coy. and T.M.Batt.	BRONFAY.	VILLE.	BRAY - MORLANCOURT.	To follow unit.	To clear Camp at 11 a.m.

1. All troops on roads East of MEAULTE (inclusive) will move in file with intervals of 200 yards between Companies and 500 yards between Battalions.

2. Troops moving on MARICOURT - BRAY road will do so at intervals of 500 yards between Companies.

3. All units whose transport is ordered to use the BERNAFAY - MARICOURT road in a Southerly direction will obtain passes to do so from A.P.M. Guards Division, in accordance with D.R.O. 1888, dated 11/12/18.

4. Special permission has been obtained from XV Corps to use the MARICOURT - BRAY road in a Southerly direction on the days of relief.

SECRET

G.D.A.
1st, 2nd, 3rd Guards Bde.
Pioneer Bn.
C.R.E.) for information.

G.D. No.2679/G.

1. The front of the XIV Corps will be re-adjusted in the near future. The exact date will be communicated as soon as it is received.

2. When the re-adjustment is completed the front will be held as follows:-

   RIGHT DIVISION from, approximately, U.20.b.9.6 to U.1.d.6.6: LEFT DIVISION thence to N.35.c.6.6.

3. G.Os.C. Right and Left Sectors and G.O.C. Guards Divnl. Artillery will at once consider the method to be adopted for holding the line under the new conditions, and report on the same.

E.Seymour
Captain,
General Staff. Guards Divn.

30th December 1916.

1st Guards Brigade.
2nd Guards Brigade.
3rd Guards Brigade.
C. R. E.
" G ".
****

Reference this Office minute No. 1130/3/A dated 26/12/16, trains have been arranged as follows :-

Date.	Train No.	From.	To.	Strength.	Time.	Unit and Strength.
Jan:2.	A.	TRONES.	PLATEAU.	1600.	load 1.00 Dep. 2.00	2/C.G. 700. 2/S.G. 700. 3rd Bde. M.G.Coy. 200 & T.M.Btty.
"	B.	"	CORBIE.	1000.	load 17.00 Dep. 18.00	2/I.G. 800. 76 Fd. Coy... 200.
Jan:3.	C.	"	PLATEAU.	700.	load 1.00 Dep. 2.00	1/I.G. 700.
"	D.	"	CORBIE.	1000.	do. do.	3/G.G. 800. 2nd Bde. M.G.Coy. 200 & T.M.Btty.
Jan:4.	E.	"	"	1700.	do. do.	1/C.G. 800. 1/S.G. 900.

B
Trains B., D., and E. will halt at PLATEAU to pick up details, but it must be clearly understood that all details must be ready to entrain at PLATEAU at the hours at which the trains are scheduled to leave TRONES WOOD and no delays there will be permitted.

H.Q., Guards Division.
29/12/16.

Major,
D.A.A.& Q.M.G., Guards Division.

S E C R E T. 　　　　　　　　　　　　　　　　1st G.B. No. 996.

2nd Bn. Grenadier Guards.	2nd Gds. Bde. M.G. Company.
1st Bn. Coldstream Guards.	1st Gds. Bde. T.M. Battery.
2nd Bn. Coldstream Guards.	2nd Gds. Bde. T.M. Battery.
3rd Bn. Coldstream Guards.	Bde., Supply Officer.
1st Bn. Irish Guards.	Bde., Transport Officer.
2nd Bn. Irish Guards.	Staff Captain.
1st Gds. Bde. M.G. Company.	Signals.

1. Herewith proposed Table of moves on relief of Guards Division by 20th Division.

2. Front line Battn's. will be relieved by Battn's. of the 61st Infantry Brigade.

3. Detailed Orders will be issued later.

4. The Division will be prepared to move to Area 3 about January 10th.

　　　　　　　　　　　　　　　　　　　　　　Captain,

27th December 1916.　　　　　　Brigade Major, 1st Guards Brigade.

MOVEMENTS OF BATTALIONS OF GUARDS DIVISION DURING RELIEF.

Date.	Unit.	From.	Destination.	Remarks.
Jany. 1st.	1/Coldstream Guards.	COMBLES Area.	LINE.	
	2/Coldstream Guards.	LINE.	BRONFAY.	Rail.
	5/Coldstream Guards.	BRONFAY.	MEAULTE.	
	2/Grenadier Guards.	BRONFAY.	MEAULTE.	
	1st Gds.Bde.M.G.Coy.	BRONFAY.	MEAULTE.	
	1st Gds.Bde.T.M.Btty.	BRONFAY.	MEAULTE.	
Jany. 2nd.	2/Irish Guards.	MALTZHORN.	CORBIE.	Rail.
	1/Irish Guards.	LINE.	BRONFAY.	Rail.
	2nd Gds.Bde.M.G.Coy.	LINE.	CORBIE.	Rail.
	2nd Gds.Bde.T.M.Btty.	LINE.	CORBIE.	Rail.
Jany. 3rd.	1/Irish Guards.	BRONFAY.	SANDPITS.	
	2/Coldstream Guards.	BRONFAY.	MEAULTE.	
	1/Coldstream Guards.	LINE.	CORBIE.	Rail.
	1st Gds.Bde. H.Q.;	LINE.	MEAULTE.	

1st Guards Brigade Intelligence Report:

8 a.m. 30th Decr. to 8 a.m. 31st Decr.

OPERATIONS.

Reliefs. 2nd Bn Coldstream Guards relieved 3rd Bn Coldstream Guards in left sub-sector - quiet relief. Relief complete 7.30 p.m.

Patrols. Four patrols went out from left Battalion during the night. No enemy met but they were seen pumping water out of their trenches and working on their wire about A 8 a 9.3. - Very lights were sent up from the Mound.

INTELLIGENCE. Right Battalion Right Coy. reports enemy trenches opposite them to be strongly held. In the evening Germans were seen helping one another home. Their trenches are apparently bad, as men are seen struggling in the mud, stuck in their trenches.

During the night a C.S.M. of the E.YORKS got into Right Battalion line having escaped from a German Prisoners Camp. The following time table of movements seen from the right battalion O.P. is given in full showing the amount of movement which can be observed almost any day.

- 8.30 a.m. Smoke of a train visible in the village of BUS. 12 men left enemy's trench in front of O.P. and went towards chalk pit which might be a dump. They returned in 5 minutes. Map reference of Dump U 9 a.
- 9.20 a.m. 8 men with coats off seen working at above dump.
- 9.25 a.m. Lamp signalling carried on for 2 minutes in enemy lines in direction of U 15 a.
- 9.40 a.m. Smoke of train seen in village of BUS.
- 9.55 a.m. Train with a 11 wagons left BUS and proceeded in direction of BARASTRE.
- 10 a.m. Enemy still visible at work in Chalk pit.
- 10.40 a.m. Four of enemy's horse transport seen on road from BUS to ROCQUIGNY appear to be heavily loaded.
- 10.45 a.m. An enemy motor lorry left ROCQUIGNY for BUS, proceeded a short distance and was met by someone on the road. It returned to ROCQUIGNY.
- 11 a.m. Large of enemy seen approaching their reserve trench opposite O.P.
- 11.15 a.m. Large amount of horse and motor trasport travelling from BUS to ROCQUIGNY and in opposite direction.
- 12.50 p.m. Men seen leaving cellars or dugouts to right of ROCQUIGNY and proceeding towards BUS.
- 1.15 p.m. From No 1 O.P. (CHURCH) saw four of enemy one apparently an Officer watching our lines for 15 minutes. They used glasses.
- 2 p.m. 1 man brought timber from rear of enemy's front trench.
- 2.15 p.m. 5 of enemy watching our lines 2 of them using glasses. They were looking towards our O.P. at 2.25 p.m. they appeared again, one with red cap to his cap pointed toward our O.P.
- 3.35 p.m. From No 2 Post (Left of support line) saw smoke from engine on left of BUS. Appears to be shunting.
- 3.40 p.m. Train left BUS and proceeded to the right, appears to be running to behind BUS.
- 3.45 p.m. About a battalion of enemy Infantry marched from the direction of BUS, and went towards BARASTRE.
- 3.50 p.m. Six men left chalk pit with equipment on, went towards wood on right rear around the village of ROCQUIGNY and the road between ROCQUIGNY and BUS seems to be heavily protected with barbed wire.

left

~~Right~~ Battalion report that Germans on their right companies front seem to want to fraternise, they waved bottles over the top and one man started to climb on to the parapet. He was shot at and fell or dropped back.

The Mound reported yesterday at O 28 c 2.4 was worked on continuously. There appears to be two dugouts here.

Small parties of Germans with packs on were seen at various times coming out of ROCQUIGNY. One small party with an Officer was lost to view going into LE MESNIL.

A motor lorry brought up metal for road repairs on the BARASTRE - BUS Road. A small party were at work on this road all day.

HOSTILE ARTILLERY.

The reserve trench of ~~reserve~~ *left* Battalion was heavily shelled from 10 a.m. to 12.30 p.m. and was considerably damaged.

Hostile artillery was very active during the morning in the neighbourhood of SAILLY CHURCH, and also about the CHATEAU. at 3 p.m. a hostile battery was seen in action at U 3 d 6.5 firing in direction of LES BOEUFS and was pointed out to the Artillery.

During the night the neighbourhood of the right battalion support line was shelled at intervals up to 1 a.m. At 12 midnight enemy artillery opened fire in response to red lights being sent up.

Fire ceased when green rockets were sent up.

OUR ARTILLERY.

At 11.45 p.m. left group apparently mistook of the green and white lights going up for an S. O. S.

Captain.
Brigade Major, 1st Guards Brigade.

S E C R E T.

Amendment to 1st Guards Brigade Order No. 95.

1st January 1917.

Reference Time Table.

Page 2. The Train for 2nd Irish Guards is timed to arrive at CORBIE at 10 P.M. Jan: 2nd.

The Train for 2nd Guards Bde. M.G.Company and T.M.Battery is timed to arrive at CORBIE at 6 A.M. Jan: 3rd.

Page 3. 1st Coldstream Guards will be relieved by 6th K.S.L.I. of 60th Infantry Brigade and not as previously stated.

Officers of 6th K.S.L.I. will be at Battn. H.Q., 1st Coldstream Guards about 1 P.M. on Jan: 2nd.

The Train for 1st Coldstream Guards is due to arrive CORBIE at 6 A.M. on Jan: 4th.

N.B. Troops moving on the MARICOURT – BRAY Road will do so at intervals of 500 yards between Coy's.

ACKNOWLEDGE.

Captain,
Brigade Major, 1st Guards Brigade.

Issued to all recipients of 1st Guards Brigade Order No. 95.

Intelligence Report, 1st Guards Brigade.

8 a.m. 31st Decr. 1916 to 1st January 1917.

OPERATIONS.

Relief. 1st Bn Irish Guards relieved 2nd Bn Irish Guards in Right sub-sector. Quiet relief. Relief complete 7.45 p.m.

Patrols. 2 N.C.O's patrols went out from left battalion, they report the German wire fairly good.
No enemy were to be seen but they were hard at work baling.

Snipers. Snipers of right battalion claim two Germans.

Prisoner. A prisoner came into the left battalion about 10.45 p.m. he had lost his way.

Aircraft. Nil.

HOSTILE ARTILLERY. Bursts of fire over SAILLY. Support line of right battalion intermittently shelled all the morning becoming intense about 2 p.m. Retaliation was called for and enemy fire ceased.

Intelligence.
At 4.30 p.m. 4 of the enemy tried to leave their trenches opposite the right of left battalion, they were fired on and went back. Ten minutes later they again tried to get out but were again fired upon. Enemy was working hard in second and third lines during the day especially in a line running on ridge in front of ROCQUIGNY from LOON COPSE to LE TRANSLOY. A certain amount of wiring was being done here.

Movements.
(a) Infantry. 7.20 a.m. 4 enemy appeared over front parapet looking towards our lines, 3 of them appeared to be Officers.
9.5 a.m. Directly in front of O.P. on Church, 2 enemy examining our line with glasses.
10.53 a.m. A party of six with stretcher bearers left the front line for rear.
12-12.30 p.m. Enemy Officers seen going in and out of front line examining our line closely with glasses.

(b) Trains and Transport.
A horse ambulance came from BUS about 9 a.m. through ROCQUIGNY to O.31.b.8.5 stretchers were put into it and the ambulance returned to BUS by the same route.
Train was seen moving in E.S.E. direction from ROCQUIGNY at 8.30 a.m., 11.30 a.m., 1.15 p.m., and 3 p.m.
At 10 a.m. Railway engine seen going into BUS. At 10.15 a.m. train with 6 wagons left BUS for LE MESNIL.
10.30 a.m. Train left BUS for BAPAUME.

Captain.
Intelligence Officer, 1st Guards Bde.

S E C R E T.   1st G.B. No. 996.

2nd Bn. Grenadier Guards.	2nd Gds. Bde. M.G. Company.
1st Bn. Coldstream Guards.	1st Gds. Bde. T.M. Battery.
2nd Bn. Coldstream Guards.	2nd Gds. Bde. T.M. Battery.
3rd Bn. Coldstream Guards.	Bde., Supply Officer.
1st Bn. Irish Guards.	Bde., Transport Officer.
2nd Bn. Irish Guards.	Staff Captain.
1st Gds. Bde. M.G. Company.	Signals.

1. Herewith proposed Table of moves on relief of Guards Division by 20th Division.

2. Front line Battn's. will be relieved by Battn's. of the 61st Infantry Brigade.

3. Detailed Orders will be issued later.

4. The Division will be prepared to move to Area 3 about January 10th.

[signature]
Captain,
27th December 1916.   Brigade Major, 1st Guards Brigade.

MOVEMENTS OF BATTALIONS OF GUARDS DIVISION DURING RELIEF.

Date.	Unit.	From.	Destination.	Remarks.
Jany. 1st.	1/Coldstream Guards.	COMBLES Area.	LINE.	
	2/Coldstream Guards.	LINE.	BRONFAY.	Rail.
	3/Coldstream Guards.	BRONFAY.	MEAULTE.	
	2/Grenadier Guards.	BRONFAY.	MEAULTE.	
	1st Gds.Bde.M.G.Coy.	BRONFAY.	MEAULTE.	
	1st Gds.Bde.T.M.Btty.	BRONFAY.	MEAULTE.	
Jany. 2nd.	2/Irish Guards.	MALTZHORN.	CORBIE.	Rail.
	1/Irish Guards.	~~BRONFAY~~ LINE.	BRONFAY.	Rail
	2nd Gds.Bde.M.G.Coy.	LINE.	CORBIE.	Rail.
	2nd Gds.Bde.T.M.Btty.	LINE.	CORBIE.	Rail.
Jany. 3rd.	1/Irish Guards.	BRONFAY.	SANDPITS.	
	2/Coldstream Guards.	BRONFAY.	MEAULTE.	
	1/Coldstream Guards.	LINE.	CORBIE.	Rail.
	1st Gds.Bde.H.Q.,	LINE.	MEAULTE.	

HANDING OVER NOTES.

Our front line lies on the forward slope of the high ground East of SAILLY SAILLISEL. The German front line varies in distance from 40 to 350 yards from our own line and is nowhere on higher ground than our own. The enemy does very little sniping either by day or by night, and the two saps opposite the Right Company of the Left Battalion although only 40 yards away appear unoccupied by day. Apparently the enemy is as busy as we are baling out and trying to make some sort of line.

Our own front line is not continuous but it is possible to visit the line held by the Left Front Company of the Right Battalion and the Right Front Company of the Left Battalion by day. There is a gap of 30 yards between the two Battalions.

As the front line is only just on the forward slope it is possible to get quite close to it without being observed by the enemy and therefore the lack of communication trenches matters less than would otherwise be the case.

There is a support trench in each Battalion Area which accommodates 1 Company of each Battalion in the line. This trench is continuous in each Battalion Area, but not between the two Battalions, where there is no trench for nearly 400 yards. Similarly there are even larger gaps between our support line and that of the Brigades on our right and left.

From the support line of the Right Battalion the ground slopes down to the front line but it is possible to get to this support line over the top without being seen.

The support line of the Left Battalion is however, lower than the front line and cannot be seen by the enemy. The enemy can observe the approach to this support line but do not interfere with individuals who pass up and down to it freely all day.

Communication/

Communication trenches are practically non-existant except for two short ones from the support to the front line in each Battalion Area. These are being improved slowly and the Pioneers are digging a new one from the Left Support Company to the CHATEAU. Communication to the CHATEAU by day is by a line of duck-boards running along the N. side of the COMBLES Valley. Another line of duck-boards runs by MOUCHOIR COPSE to the CHATEAU but this is in view from LE TRANSLOY and must not be used by day.

The Advanced Brigade Dump is at the CHATEAU, which pack animals and carrying parties can reach by day. The main Dump is at HAIE Wood where wagons unload and where the DECANVILLE Railway ends.

Rations are brought up by rail to COMBLES (Western edge of Village), where they are met by pack animals and delivered to the Battalion in COMBLES the day before it is due to go into the trenches.

Pack animals are kept in COMBLES and are allotted by Brigade H.Q., daily for distributing rations and taking stores and material up to the line. Pack animals are supplemented by 5 extra horses from each Battalion in the Group which also remain in COMBLES.

Two Companies are used each morning from the COMBLES Battalion for taking up stores and material to CHATEAU Dump.

Work is being carried out as follows :-

<u>Front Battn's.</u> (a) Maintenance of existing trenches.

      (b) Extension of support line inwards so as to meet and become continuous.

      (c) Wiring of all lines.

<u>The R.E.</u> - are employed on 5 strong points sited with a view to defending our right flank. Three of these are finished i.e. SAILLY in Right Battalion Support Line garrisoned by Right Battalion - SOUTH COPSE garrisoned by COMBLES Battalion and COMBLES at present occupied by the Trench Mortar Battery.

- 3 -

A Tunnelling Company is making accommodation for another Company at HAIE Wood and is improving the accommodation at the QUARRY.

The Pioneers are digging a communication trench from Left Support Company H.Q., U.8.c.5.8. to the CHATEAU along the Western outskirts of SAILLY SAILLISEL.

There is one good Observation Post in each Battalion area.

The Artillery have a Liaison Officer at each Battalion H.Q., by night. By day these Officers are supposed to be in their O.P's. but they are short of these.

Areas chiefly shelled are :-
    SAILLY Church -
    PERONNE - BAPAUME Road -
    QUARRY -
    Reserve Line Left Battalion -
    COMBLES Cemetery.

Captain,
31st Dec: 1916.   Brigade Major, 1st Guards Brigade.

Please destroy Instructions No 5 for Right Group at present in your possession.

SECRET.   1st G.B. No.801/5/1.

2nd Bn. Grenadier Guards.   3rd Bn. Coldstream Guards.
1st Bn. Coldstream Guards.   1st Bn. Irish Guards.
2nd Bn. Coldstream Guards.   2nd Bn. Irish Guards.

AMENDED INSTRUCTIONS NO. 5 FOR RIGHT GROUP.

Subject :- MISCELLANEOUS.

CLEAN CLOTHING.

1. Units will indent on the Sanitary Officer on the day on which they move in to the COMBLES Area, for the number of suits of clean underclothing, socks, etc., which they require the day their Unit comes out of the line.

    It is essential that Units should indent for clean clothing for the bare number of men actually in the trenches. Attention is drawn to the Major Generals circular on the subject of the return of dirty clothing.

    Units will have to send for their clothing and also return the dirty to the Laundry.

MULES.

2. Twelve mules are allotted for the use of Battn's. the day they move into the line. Battn's. will notify Group H.Q., of the time and place at which they require these mules to parade. These mules are available to take any load as may be directed by the Battn., concerned up to the CHATEAU. They should not start from HAIE Wood later than 2-30 P.M.

WATER.

3. On the evening of their arrival in COMBLES, Battn's. will notify Group H.Q., of the number of Petrol Tins required to take up water to the line the next day.

    A party will be sent to draw these Tins from the Gum Boots Store at 10 A.M. on the day on which Battn's. move into the line.

    They will then be filled in COMBLES and sent up to the line under Battn. arrangements.

    On coming out of the line Battn's. will bring back ALL their empty tins and dump them at the Gum Boot Store and obtain a receipt for the total number of tins returned.

    (a) The present arrangement of supplying water to HAIE Wood is found to be unsatisfactory, and is cancelled. The following arrangements will be substituted :-

    (b) The water butts at HAIE Wood will no longer be used, but full petrol tins will be brought up daily to HAIE Wood under Brigade arrangements, and be handed over to Sgt. DANKS, Brigade Dump, who will issue them on the following scale :-

    25 tins for Company at HAIE Wood, coming in about 4 PM.
    25 tins for Company at T.18.Central, coming in about 4 PM.
    35 tins for M.G.Company at HAIE Wood and in the line.
    12 tins for "X" Guards T.M.Battery.
    15 tins for Details and Sgt. Danks.

    Receipts will be given for all water issued and empty tins will be returned on the following day not later than 1 PM. at which hour the next supply will have arrived. Care will be taken that the full number of empty tins is returned daily.

(c)/

(c) Battalions going into the trenches will as now draw empty tins from the Store in COMBLES, fill them and carry them on their limber to HAIE Wood. These will be returned empty to COMBLES when the Battn., is relieved. Receipts will in all cases be given at the Store. There is a maximum number of 100 tins available for issue to any one Battalion.

(d) Battalions in the trenches requiring more water the second night will be supplied with not more than 50 full tins at HAIE Wood: empty tins will be brought down in exchange. Notice must be given by 2 P.M. the day they are required.

(e) The working of this system depends entirely on the correct return of empty tins. All tins will be care-:fully salvaged and a report will be sent to this Office by any Unit returning a less number than it drew from the Store at COMBLES or at HAIE Wood.

(f) This system will come into force to-morrow, 24th inst.,

R.E. MATERIAL.

4. From 19th inst., all R.E. Material will be drawn by Battn's. in the line from a new Brigade Dump which has been established near the duck-boards just S.W. of the CHATEAU. This Dump will be in charge of Group H.Q., Indents for R.E. Material will be sent in in the usual way i.e. by 8 P.M. The Storeman will live at Battn., H.Q., at the CHATEAU.

Parties drawing from this Dump will hand a chit signed by the Adjutant of their Unit to the Storeman. It would save much time and labour if Battn's. would inform the Storeman beforehand of what they intend to draw. The necessary Stores can then be made up in separate lots.

100 Duck-boards will be brought up each morning to CHATEAU Dump. Each Battalion in front line will be able to draw 50 of these Duck-boards, for use in their line. More will be supplied each day if possible, but the above number is a minimum. Any Duck-boards above this number brought to CHATEAU Dump will also be divided equally between right and left Battn's.

The Battn's. concerned will be notified, if possible, of the number above 50 which they may draw.

23rd December 1916.

Captain,
Brigade Major, 1st Guards Brigade.

SECRET.   1st G.B. No.801/6.

2nd Bn. Grenadier Guards.   3rd Bn. Coldstream Guards.
1st Bn. Coldstream Guards.   1st Bn. Irish Guards.
2nd Bn. Coldstream Guards.   2nd Bn. Irish Guards.

INSTRUCTIONS NO.6 FOR RIGHT GROUP.

Subject :- COMBLES Trench.

1. The accommodation in COMBLES Trench and in the shelters to the South, leaves much to be desired. Every effort will therefore be made by each Battalion to improve the accommodation.

2. A work party will be detailed every morning by the Battalion in COMBLES to work on the trench and on the shelters, under the supervision of an R.E. N.C.O.

3. Advanced parties of incoming Companies will reach Company H.Q., COMBLES Trench not later than 12-30 P.M. to take over -
    (a) the shelters available.   (d) the blankets
    (b) the scheme of work on improvements.
    (c) the tools and stores.

4. Every effort will be made to collect the salvage lying round the trench: this will be taken to the Brigade Dump outside Brigade H.Q., in COMBLES.

5. The vicinity of the trench will be kept clean. Refuse and tins will be buried. Proper latrines will be built.

6. New material and salvaged material for improvements is available.

7. All unserviceable blankets will be collected and handed in to the Gum Boot Store in COMBLES where a receipt will be obtained.

Care will be taken that blankets are kept dry and not trodden into the mud.

                                                           Captain,
20th Decr. 1916.   Brigade Major, 1st Guards Brigade.

SECRET.   1st G.B. No.801/7.

    2nd Bn. Grenadier Guards.   1st Bn. Irish Guards.
    1st Bn. Coldstream Guards.   2nd Bn. Irish Guards.
    2nd Bn. Coldstream Guards.   75th Coy., R.E.
    3rd Bn. Coldstream Guards.   Company H.Q., T.18.Central.

INSTRUCTIONS NO.7 FOR RIGHT GROUP.

Subject :- Dugout accommodation in T.18.Central -
            near Intermediate Line.

1.   This accommodation is new and improvements are immediately necessary. These improvements will be carried out, under R.E. supervision, by the garrison and will be continuous.

2.   The following work will be undertaken at once :-

  (a)   Laying a duck-board track from the main track up the side of each row of dug-outs. Each Company will draw every morning from the Brigade Dump at HAIE Wood at least 30 duck-boards and place them in position.

  (b)   Digging a drain alongside the line of duck-boards: a drain will be dug round the roof of each dugout, connecting up with the main drain.

  (c)   Elephant irons will be drawn as available from the HAIE Wood Dump and the proper roofing of the dugouts will be undertaken.

3.   A field oven has been constructed, and Companies will in future arrange for their own cooking on the spot. Fuel will be supplied by the Battalion concerned. The cooker at present at HAIE Wood for the use of the Company in T.18.Central will be withdrawn.

4.   25 petrol tins of water will be at HAIE Wood for the use of the Company on its arrival.

5.   All wet and unserviceable blankets will be returned to the Brigade Dump at HAIE Wood, and a receipt obtained. Blankets will not be used as shelters for door-ways, etc.,

6.   Proper latrines will be made.

7.   Advanced parties of incoming Company will reach Company H.Q., T.18.Central not later than 3 P.M. to take over :-

  (a)   The shelters available.
  (b)   The scheme of work on improvements.
  (c)   The blankets.
  (d)   The tools.

    Receipts will be given for (c) and (d), copies of which will be called for from time to time.

                                                        Captain,

23rd December 1916.   Brigade Major, 1st Guards Brigade.

6 Bn. Sapping platoons.
Sgt Parkinson

1st G.B. No. 898

Right Group.

Instructions for Sapping Platoons.

1. The Sapping Platoons are now accommodated in two Groups -

    Group A.   DOG, ASS, BIRD trenches T.27.d.
    2/G.G., 1/C.G., 2/C.G., 1/I.G.,

    Group B.   COMBLES T.28.b.
    3/C.G., 2/I.G.,

2. The senior Officer in each Group will be responsible -

    (a) that the dugouts and shelters are kept properly clean. Officers must inspect their dugouts and shelters daily.

    (b) that proper latrines are made for each Platoon.

    (c) that the vicinity of the shelters is kept clean and clear of all refuse and excreta.

    (d) that improvements to shelters are continuous - men will be detailed by the Brigade for this work.

3. Sergeant PARKINSON, 2nd Bn. Coldstream Guards has been appointed Acting Quarter Master Sergeant to the six Platoons. He will draw the rations from the Train and see that they are properly distributed to the various Platoons. He should report at once to O.C., Platoons if their rations are not complete. He will employ any spare men left behind in clearing and in general improvements.

4. The Acting Quartermaster Sergeant will obtain from Officers and render to Brigade H.Q., every other day the fighting strength of each Platoon.

5. One N.C.O. or old soldier and a cook should be left behind in charge of kit and shelters by each Platoon.

    The senior Officer in Group A will detail two men as permanent sanitary men; the senior Officer in Group B will similarly detail one man.

6. All salvage - greatcoats, rifles, equipment, etc., must be collected and put in the Dump outside Brigade H.Q.,

7. All gum boots not in use must be returned at once to the Gum Boot Store in COMBLES, and a receipt obtained for them.

8/

- 2 -

8. Care must be taken that no men other than those detailed in para. 5 are left behind.

9. Casualties should be reported at once to Brigade H.Q., who will report to the Battalion concerned.

10. Blankets must be carefully looked after: they must not be used for covering shelters. All unserviceable blankets must be returned at once to the Gum Boot Store in COMBLES, and a receipt obtained for them there.

Captain,
Brigade Major, 1st Guards Brigade.

20th Decr. 1916.

www.ingramcontent.com/pod-product-compliance
Lightning Source LLC
Chambersburg PA
CBHW051527190426
43193CB00045BA/2247